Ministry Mechanics

Christopher W. Perkins

Ministry Mechanics

ISBN 978-1506-900-44-5 PRINT

LCCN 2015954109

October 2015

Published and Distributed by

First Edition Design Publishing, Inc.

P.O. Box 20217, Sarasota, FL 34276-3217

www.firsteditiondesignpublishing.com

Table of Contents

CHAPTER 1

Introduction

My reasons for authoring this book.

When I became a Christian, the call to follow Jesus was intense. A decision to become a disciple, as I have found through scripture, involves a number of costs to count such as giving your life, purpose and loyalty to God. In my twenty plus years as a disciple of Jesus, I have found that many believers have circumvented the Luke 14:25-33 and Luke 9:26 requirement to see if they truly have the character to do what it takes to become a devoted follower of Jesus.

My reason for writing this book is to educate and encourage those who profess leadership in God's modern-day church to take a closer look at how they are structuring their respective churches and/ or specific ministries, facilitate a greater understanding of how to draw closer to God in a spiritual community that aspires to share the same endeavor, help those who are lost find salvation, and support those who have found their hope in God as they stay faithful and resolute.

I will attempt to explain in simple, pragmatic terms and examples how to build an understandable, spiritual and social infrastructure which a church or specific ministry can build upon for greater effectiveness and fruitfulness.

Those leaders who allow themselves to be challenged and encouraged by this writing will find a number of ministry myths dispelled so that leading no longer has to be an issue of luck or walking in the dark. Many ministers, who themselves are untrained for the work they are commissioning, send others out with little more than "a hope and a prayer" that the novice will succeed in a place of ministry he or she has no idea what to do with. For those with a heart to learn and be challenged (Acts 17:10-12), this writing is for you.

I have also written this work as a guide and reference tool usable as subjectively as you like based entirely on your specific situation. This is not a "how to" or "paint by the numbers" book of ministry that addresses every problem and answers every question. The purpose of this writing is to facilitate, for you the reader, a greater understanding of the "process" that your endeavors toward ministry will need to undergo. In essence, I am—metaphorically speaking—giving you a lump of clay: providing you with some simple tools and perspectives and letting you come up with the shape and design.

I have seen several ministers and church leaders use some of my concepts very loosely and make some of my suggestions their own by implementing certain strategies intertwined with their own personality and style. These practitioners enjoyed a greater degree of success than they had previously achieved. Most untrained leaders, to whom I am primarily writing, need only a nudge in the right direction or a timely piece of advice in order to improve their ministry. When one is mired in the depths and complexities of his or her specific ministry situation, some very specific and pragmatic bits of advice can be of great value (proverbs 15:23 NIV).

CHAPTER 2

Some Basic Questions

What I expect in return

God's kingdom led by the most prepared, noble-hearted people possible. This book was a suggestion by close friends and colleagues, but the content therein is a compilation of over 20 years' experience as a ministry leader, trainer, architect, and advisor. I am honored, privileged, and humbled that God would allow me to share some of the highlights of my ministry experiences. I hope to enrich the lives of so many who aspire to lead in God's service. This writing I joyfully offer to those who could benefit from a study of my personal journey, delivered in a pragmatic, user-friendly, and un-proprietary way.

What my vision is for this book

My vision is to see a robust synergy thrive within churches and specific ministries—whether independent or within a larger corporate church – by giving Christian believers a fighting chance to prepare, in their respective folds, for the days to come in service for God.

Who I believe should study this book

Anyone who aspires to lead in God's service regardless of specific duties could benefit from the contents of this book.

CHAPTER 3

Explanation and Disclaimer

This writing is not exhaustive. I intend this book to be an informative work that addresses a variety of issues one may encounter while managing a church or ministry. In future writings I plan to deal with topics on a more in-depth, three dimensional way, so that readers will be able to reference detailed case studies on topics of interest such as evangelism, appointing an assistant leader, dealing with disunity, and navigating co-ed leadership dynamics. Here I attempt to give general expositions for each topic and provide a helpful, user-friendly tutorial to motivate your own creative and scholastic endeavors.

The main reason for my decision to go only to this level of discourse is that I want to avoid "information overload". For the new, frustrated, or "stuck in a rut" leader who wants creative and pragmatic solutions to the myriad intricacies involved in pursuing a ministry, I designed the style and chose the content of this book with you in mind.

I will put forth subsequent works by which we can delve deeper into the sub- topics of the issues covered in this book, but my goal at this juncture is to establish some elementary concepts related to the basic principles of ministry-building.

Thank you for letting me share in your ministry journey as a guest.

To God Be the Glory!
Christopher W. Perkins

What is the reality now?

What started out as an exciting and clear-cut plan to change the world/ community/ family/ neighborhood/ city/ and so forth has unexpectedly become complicated, heavy, confusing and discouraging. " My closest advisors and subordinate leaders have taken things in their own direction, seem to resent any feedback or discipling I try to give and flounder in their respective ministries—but never seek or want any significant input. People come in to our ministry excited and loyal but leave quietly, lukewarm, discouraged, or just plain disinterested," a troubled leader may say to themselves.

Though this might not be the specific state of your ministry or church, you might find parallels between your situation and the scenario sketched above. One must always have the courage to ask the question with regard to your current ministry situation, "What is the reality now?". Many will deceive themselves by covering up the present reality with their ideal vision and consoling themselves with the delusional assumption that "God will work out the details" while they sit back and do nothing about their dilemmas.

Though God does work in all situations, a helpful study of the Book of Proverbs yields insight into God's attitude toward a disciple doing his part to learn and grow. Many stories of characters in the Bible as well as the overall book of Proverbs would suggest that God is not interested in shortcutting anything or cushioning anyone from the blows of hard lessons that one will need to learn in order to refine him or her first as a person of God and then as a leader in God's service. For example, if a person is overweight and wants to get into shape, JUST imagining that he or she could one day look like one of the cover models of Shape or GQ magazine is not going to be enough. If a person is in debt, just imagining the day when he or she will miraculously have that significant surplus of funds and the discipline to manage them will not be enough.

CHAPTER 4

What should be three general goals for your ministry?

To Grow

I specify the number three because it is the number I work with best when I have to manage different situations simultaneously. If I have a number of things to work on, I try to pick three of the most important or pressing issues and tackle those first. As you adapt my strategies for your own use, decide what your effective "multitasking threshold" is and go from there.

Some leaders start a ministry or multiple ministries with the goal of cultivating a following and enlarging their membership with an ultimate aim toward enhancing their parishioners' spiritual growth through creative means. The goal usually starts out fairly clear-cut and simple, but leaders sometimes become too embroiled in the intricacies involved in the process of attaining that goal without empowering others to help. Because of these variables, they lose their way, become distracted, disillusioned, or just outright discouraged. Some struggle with a combination of all these states. Each leader's preparation and ability to manage the process will determine the degree of success he or she attains.

A conviction I have gained through many years of doing this kind of work is that the journey and process are more important than attaining the goal. Some might try to attain many goals as a ministry leader without taking into account that goals change, grow and evolve and that attaining a goal sets one up to have to maintain it (i.e. membership growth, financial prosperity, new ministries, and so forth). The experienced leader focuses more on his or her ability to learn from and manage the "process" rather than on the result. My point is not that goals are unimportant but that one must also strive for a proper balance between focusing on the process and focusing on the result.

To Strengthen

Ministry leaders need to be very strong Biblically since knowledge of God will be the foundation upon which everything else will be built. Leaders must be strong of character, resolved in the pursuit of their goals, and flexible enough to navigate the random variables that will present themselves at unforeseen times. Leaders also need a strong network of peers who will support them. More importantly, leaders must feel emboldened and empowered enough to speak frankly and honestly about any given situation. This can be very challenging since many oversight or "senior" leaders develop a propensity to insulate themselves from those who would offer a strong, qualified critique or disagree with their opinions. Strong leaders should beware of surrounding themselves with sycophantic "yes men," Though to cultivate flattery feels better and has short-term advantages; the long-term results will be disastrous.

To Deepen Spiritually

The ministry leader or leaders must display a knowledgeable command of the Bible, a solid prayer life, and a disciplined and principle-centered lifestyle. Being strong in these matters but approachable will be staple characteristics of a potentially successful leader. Most men are not like this naturally; consequently, those leaders with these qualities should have the conviction that part of their mandate is to train men of good character. As we see in Paul's letters to Timothy (Especially in 2 Timothy 2:2 where Paul exhorts

Timothy to specifically teach other reliable and trustworthy men all that he [Paul] taught him [Timothy]), Paul instills morality in Timothy and disciples him to be everything he needs to be in order to attain success in his ministry.

CHAPTER 5

Assessing the Shortcomings of Your Ministry

The following points in this segment deal with some very troubling and intimate questions we can find ourselves asking when the vision we had for our ministry seems to be getting lost.

Many times we become so troubled, confused or just discouraged that we not only fail to ask these tough questions with the drive and desire to find solutions, but avoid them altogether.

My challenge for you, the reader, is to be able to sort through the different shortcomings in your ministry, analyze and solve allowing yourself to be tested by God.

Remember the story of Solomon in 1 Kings 3:1-15 where Solomon was approached by God. When Solomon had the opportunity to advance his own wealth, he chose instead a greater wisdom and discerning of heart by which to both serve and govern God's people. Even the greatest leaders ask for help when faced with tough situations.

Don't be afraid to face the inevitable challenges of leading and never be afraid to ask God and others for wisdom and help.

I caution against letting your heart choose the all-too-common path of "denial" and obstinence as a way to deal with ministry shortcomings. Let yourself be helped. Don't be afraid to let people know that you need and want help.

Why are we not growing anymore?

Was growth a problem from the start of your ministry? Did growth happen quickly for a time and then lose momentum? Are there areas where the current ministry infrastructure (or lack thereof) seems to be breaking down? Are the established mechanisms and protocols so rigid and inflexible that although once very useful in the overall maintenance and tempo, they have become obsolete and/ or inapplicable and have put a "chokehold" on future potential for growth and fluidity? Is there a growing spirit of discouragement and unrest consuming the ministry? Be honest when facing these questions and the questions in the following sections because as one evolves in maturity and depth, he will see growth in his ministry situation only by addressing problem areas.

Why are we not deepening spiritually?

What is the axis or "spiritual linchpin" that holds together the different components that comprise your ministry's infrastructure? Do you have a comprehensive mission and strategy for meeting important benchmarks, or is every component of your ministry handled catch-as-catch can? Consider components of your ministry infrastructure such as spiritual vernacular, business communication, mission/vision, application, execution and enforcement. What is the cohesive bond holding all parts together?

In many cases, reassessing the individual components of your ministry's foundation and the process by which that foundation is established can yield clear insight into current and possibly future problems. Another method of assessing structural deficiencies is to identify a person who has some knowledge of ministry mechanics and expertise but is not too sentimentally or emotionally tied to the ministry in question to make objective observations. Request of this person to make an unsentimental diagnosis of the prevailing problems and challenges he or she sees facing the ailing ministry. This person can be from either inside or outside of the congregation but must be able to view the situation from an unbiased vantage point. In general, a ministry leader would be an inappropriate choice for this role because the person being evaluated would have to be receptive to findings possibly unflattering to his or her leadership. Unfortunately, pride and arrogance are not the downfall only of many Christian leaders, but of their ministries as well and hold many back from capitalizing on great opportunities presented from such critiques given by others. If self-preservation and love of self-image come before drawing one's ministry closer to God, leadership (or at least in its present form) might not be the most prudent place for such a person.

How is a lack of Discipline hurting my ministry?

Discipline is a much-underrated component and virtue among many leaders and their ministries. So many modern Christians approach spiritual growth and development from a very emotional and compulsive disposition and view discipline as an obstacle that compares unfavorably to a more charismatic style characterized by dogmatism and mysticism. However, to cultivate or improve any area of life—marriage, health, career, child-rearing, finances, home making, and so forth—requires a disciplined approach. It is ironic that the modern-day church and many of its subordinate ministries so willingly dismiss discipline as worldly, legalistic, and in some cases a denial of God's Holy Spirit, who is often equated solely with intense emotional or spiritual compulsion, when scripture clearly posits discipline as a fundamental feature of discipleship. For example, Paul states in several passages, "he beat his body and made it his slave, he endured hardships of many kinds, he became all things to all men in hopes that he might win a few" (I Cor. 9:27, 2 Tim. 2:10,I Cor. 9:19 respectively NIV.) Paul uses his sense of self-discipline as a weapon for God in advancing his ministry. Unfortunately, many leaders run their ministry in as undisciplined a fashion as they run their personal lives. Men can only and truly lead as they are. It is difficult to lead from a position one has not attained with any integrity. If one puts on a show of discipline just for public performance but does not lead a genuinely principled life, it will not be long before the character deficiency begins to have an adverse effect on the overall ministry. This dynamic becomes apparent regardless of a superficial and insincere display of organization and discipline.

Another destructive dynamic pertaining to a lack of discipline in leadership is that it replicates itself in subordinates who also struggle with a lack of discipline. In time, this will consume and ultimately destroy a ministry or ministries. In Proverbs 20:4, we see that "harvest time" becomes very scarce if the hard work needed during "planting" is not taken seriously or expeditiously. Frantic and "busy" activity in general is not a substitute for the specific hard work needed to run a ministry if a leader desires God-pleasing growth and life. Worrying about something but never specifically doing anything about the problem never brings about any adequate solutions.

I am worried about the growing spirit of disunity.

Without a set foundation and well-planned, executed and enforced infrastructural paradigm, many in the ministry will become discontent with the lack of organization and progress in their ministry and implement their own plan or vision. Consequently, they will design and follow their own modus operandi. If not handled forcefully and expeditiously, disunity can obliterate ministries on all levels. See the biblical story of the Exodus regarding the golden calf. In Exodus 32:1-35, Moses went to the top of Sinai to receive further plans from God. In his short time away from the camp, the people began a revolt fueled by impatience, lack of faith and disobedience. Aaron was left in charge by Moses and gave in to the "mob" by creating a golden image of a calf for the people to worship. Lack of mission, lack of leadership and lack of very specific instruction gave way to absolute disunity and anarchy. This group of people who lacked such faith were the very people who had just witnessed the parting of the Red Sea and crossed it on dry ground! Never assume unity in your ministry. Unity takes great effort, thought and discipline to have as a core component of your ministry.

How do I think through a strategic plan?

A simple, attainable vision will help to determine a course of action. Leave nothing to chance with regard to what you would like to accomplish and how you will attain those goals. God and his Holy Spirit will provide more than enough surprises to keep you humble and refined in spirit. Once again, so many areas of life—marriage, career, finance, competition, and so forth—are acknowledged to demand discipline and planning, yet ministry work is often approached in a haphazard way wherein the leader relies on emotion and inspiration but lacks the balance of advance planning and the discipline to carry out those plans. At this end of the spectrum is a ministry characterized by overdependence on the emotional, visionary, and a "just follow your heart and God will take care of the rest" mentality. At the opposite end is a ministry rendered uninspired and task-oriented by too much planning and discipline and too little emotion or joy. Through prayer and the cultivation of a circle of honest relationships with people who feel they can be very frank and honest (Ecclesiastes 7:16-18), you can maintain a favorable balance between these two extremes.

If I am flexible, does that show a weakness in my planning?

Never be afraid of tweaking a plan or strategy if it is not working. Depending on your goals and visions, what worked for you in another ministry or what worked for someone else might not work out the same for you. Differing membership demographics, contexts, cultures and other variables can and should determine how you will plan and execute your ministry. I have found over the years that although characteristics vary from one ministry to another, over time and through work, study, and trial-and-error, an experienced and flexible leader will discover the style or system best suited to the prevailing situation.

For example, if robust evangelism is a goal I have for a ministry (a very simple, Biblical, attainable goal), it will have different manifestations in my strategic plan depending on what ministry I am leading: in a youth or campus ministry, I would use different strategies to motivate constituencies, set goals, establish tempo, and maintain day-to-day operations than I would use in the context of a married ministry or a single-parent ministry. Keep in mind, though, that the overall plan and vision for a robust evangelism should be universal and bind the various ministries together in a coherent way.

Other ministries will have their own unique challenges. Be flexible, find as many common denominators as possible (such as, but certainly not limited to, evangelism as in the example above), then discover the peculiar differences and subtle nuances in each ministry. Then figure out how to be successful in that particular ministry.

In conclusion to this segment, these are just a few examples of concerning thoughts a leader may come across at any given time. As you may think of more, try to understand the process by which I thought through the problem rather than specific solutions.

CHAPTER 6

Selling People on Your Ministry

Sometimes the hardest people to sell the value of your ministry to are the Christians in your own church. In a world of oversaturation, overstimulation, and the sheer volume of options, people have become desensitized to important issues. People hear or receive invitations to ministry events such as a Bible discussions or Sunday school classes and immediately feel burdened with attending "just another activity." Most believers have a great attitude and intend to be supportive of the corporate directive to attend the various ministry events. However, people can begin to "tune out" after a while because of the number of events. They become numb to a ministry process that has gone from unique to commonplace and where quality of ministry activity options is replaced by quantity and volume. By keeping your ministry simple in its core values and focus, even with multiple strategies in place to meet the needs of a ministry's various demographic constituents, one can continue to highlight and promote special ministry events with great effect and success. The age old concept of "less is more" cannot be over stated.

For example, if the core mission of the corporate body is evangelistic growth and leadership development, every church ministry within the corporate body will be able to support this larger mission at the local level. Building upon a common scriptural foundation and philosophy, church members can simply shift over into new ministry roles more suitable to themselves without having to learn a completely new ministry vernacular or paradigm. If all ministries endeavor to share the same fundamentals of scriptural communication or "vernacular" as I refer to it, switching a ministry becomes more of a subtle, cosmetic shift rather than a completely disorienting paradigm shift that would adversely affect all levels of ministry, including core foundational values.

Without a simple, scripturally cohesive theme that ties the corporate body together at all levels, each ministry will be guided by the diverse ideas, cultures and backgrounds of each ministry leader. This lack of cohesion can cause a perpetual tide of differentiation starting at the ministry's sub-divisional level and compounding throughout the corporate structure. This dynamic will ultimately result in chaos. The greater a church grows in membership numbers in absence of a cohesive strategic plan (and the discipline to adhere to it), the more difficult it will become to manage divergent doctrinal, personal, and exegetical philosophies. The corporate body is then ripe for implosion.

One of the most ineffectual mechanisms ministries put in place—albeit with the best of intentions—is man-made protocols, which after time crystallize to such a degree that they become a law unto themselves and lack the ability to allow a ministry to develop, ripen, and flourish organically.

Persevere through gentle persistence.

If your ministry wants to change its core mission and foundational direction, that difficult work will demand that leadership persuade the membership of all ministries at all levels to embrace the new philosophical paradigm. This work must be undertaken patiently and methodically, and after careful analysis, it should be accompanied by systematic simplification. People will need the space and freedom to question and disagree. It is leadership's responsibility to remain consistent in gently and persistently pressing for the new changes and ushering people into agreement. The leadership team must have strong leadership oversight of its own to sustain its motivation over what might amount to a very long and difficult journey. Speed and a forceful hand will not determine long-term success and viability as much as gentle persistence and graceful fortitude will. Proverbs 16:32 (NIV) sums up perfectly the type of wisdom one will need based on propensity to deal with the paradigm shift a ministry may need to undergo. Many leaders become impatient giving way to over lording, legalism and harshness. In accordance with this particular scripture, pray for the strength to choose the path of patient and loving wisdom over force of will and dictatorship. Cultural change within the church is a subtle and lengthy battle that most leaders avoid for some of these reasons as well as others.

How do I get help?

Whether you are a leadership team or an individual, you will need help from a number of sources. Remember that the ultimate source needs to be the Bible. Knowledge of scripture will always deliver fruit. Relationships with people are useful and essential, but ultimately subjective and based on fallible human nature. Make sure all of your decisions have a solid scriptural base; be flexible; and get ready for the battle. There might be many times when you will have to stand alone.

We have large attendances to services. Does that mean we are evangelistically healthy?

Amidst the chaos and disorder of trying to unify the various ministries that make up your corporate body, you still have the God-given responsibility to keep the evangelistic fervor and mission of the ministry moving consistently in a forward direction. The fact that a church or local ministry has a large number of visitors attending—even if that large number of visitors is consistent due to the successful mass marketing of ministry programs and music (which do have their place)—does not necessarily mean that it is an evangelistically healthy church. In both large and small corporate church settings, it is easy to hide behind a growth strategy that leaves evangelism primarily to a marketing department or specific ministry dedicated exclusively to evangelism. Evangelism is the fruit of a healed life. It is a great disservice to the Christians in your ministry on all levels to impede their growth by not encouraging and discipling them in how to live a lifestyle of evangelism. I am often reminded of Paul's charge and encouragement in Philemon 1:4-7 when he gives the charge to be active in sharing our faith which keeps us focused on all the good that God is and does. Evangelism was designed by God to keep our hearts soft towards Him by keeping us focused on speaking about Him to others. Evangelism was not some marketing scheme or campaign invented by some random minister. Churches that shortcut the evangelical process by using marketing teams or firms to handle this aspect of their mission perpetuate a subtle process of spiritual erosion. Though invisible at first, mediocrity and lack of depth and zeal will eventually consume the corporate body. Spiritual erosion will also impede the growth of God's kingdom whether the church in question numbers ten or ten thousand. In the book of Revelation chapters 2-3, a number of large, established and metropolitan churches had lost their focus and zeal for God while excelling in worldly and community endeavors. These churches were allegedly materialistically successful according to evidences in scripture. Yet even amidst the worldly accomplishments, God admonishes them for their lack of heart for Him. Ultimately, relationships are what tie a group together. Deep abiding relationships are an essential component in nurturing a heart that desires God and maintaining spiritual harmony in a large or small group ministry. Busywork, activities and dynamic entertainment (regardless of how spiritual one might think that entertainment is) cannot substitute for deep and spiritually intimate relationships individually and collectively. As far as entertainment and marketing schemes as your sole source of evangelism, eventually, another church or ministry will catch on to its competitor's strategy and use those tactics to lure away its competitor's following. Competition to stage the best "show" in town then cheapens the spiritual and evangelical mission and membership simply becomes a revolving with Christians going from church to church looking for the "flavor of the month" in regards to the "spiritual" entertainment aspect of "worship".

CHAPTER 7

How Do I Salvage What Is Left Of My Ministry?

Every ministry has some kind of structure built in whether by design or chance.

Keep in mind that no structure at all is in and of itself a "structure". I have seen many ministers who are "vision-heavy", meaning they see something they want to accomplish (many times based on successes they have seen others attain) and set forth equipped with inspiration and "faith" alone in order to achieve those desired results. Much like the "compulsive shopper", they want what they really cannot afford at this time. The problem with such a two-dimensional approach is that time and the many unforeseeable variables that come with building that ministry vision begin to erode the initial feelings of inspirational euphoria—that "I-can- conquer-the-world-with-God-on-my-side" feeling. Failing to set goals and devise a strategy for implementing them and evaluating progress compounds the initial problems stemming from the lack of balance in the initial approach. This being contrary to those who take the time think things through to their logical conclusion. Even as they ride the wave of inspiration and emotion, they will harvest sweeter fruit waiting along the way than those who do not think their plan through logically. Lack of planning is not faith. In Proverbs 19:2, we see that zeal, emotion and excitement cannot be the main driver behind a lasting commensurate of any substance. One must possess wisdom to balance and anchor all of that energy as well.

Every ministry has some kind of vision.

Most potential or experienced leaders embarking on a ministry endeavor aspire to pursue something specific through their prospective ministries. While each individual's goals will vary, the concepts discussed in this writing are universal in that they posit strategies for reaching a ministry goal in a logical, efficient, spiritual and sustainable way.

Where do you go when you have exhausted ideas on how to grow the ministry?

Besides praying and studying the Bible, let the people in your ministry be your guide and sounding board. Most ministries are full of creative and hard-working people just waiting for an opportunity to exercise their own creative ability in service to God. Be secure and mature enough to understand that others around you in your ministry (who may not even be leaders) may have more pertinent ideas on certain aspects of the ministry. Give others around you a chance to dream and contribute as well, so that others gain a sense of ownership by sharing the vision-creating process. A leader who adopts this strategy will grow a circle of trusted advisers who have a personal stake in the ministry endeavor's future viability. Collect all the great ideas and see what resonates in your own spirit and the hearts of your council members. I would highly recommend that a ministry leader seek advice from those who "intimidate" him because they seem to possess a great deal of wisdom in areas where he would like to grow. Every ministry has people like this—people who come with a respectable amount of ministry knowledge and experience an insecure ministry leader tends to avoid.

Reaching out to such members will help a ministry leader overcome feelings of intimidation while fostering a relationship based on humility and gaining fresh ideas about how to take the ministry in different directions.

Can I do this alone or should I consider finding others to help me?

Surrounding oneself with helpful and even challenging advisors must be a principle-centered conviction from the start. Anyone who feels that he can do it alone or has the belief that he must always be the center of all decisions (or attention) should really consider his motives and the overall condition of his heart and spirit in connection with the matter and reconsider how to proceed with a change of heart and attitude.

"I feel alone in this ministry". How does a leader find people they can talk to?

Those in more subordinate roles of ministry leadership—facilitators and administrators, for example—will need to have supportive advisors around them as well so as to ensure that all communication with their oversight leader is open, honest, encouraging and visionary. A spirit of cooperation will be essential in overcoming feelings of insecurity. The strategies I am describing in this segment can sometimes be difficult to implement due to all-too-human personality conflicts often between leaders. If that is the case, it is my personal conviction that one can overcome that obstacle by examining his motives with an aim toward maintaining a pure heart and conscience before God. No situation (regardless of how spiritually ambitious or successful it may seem) is worth compromising one's own convictions to the detriment of his soul. I take seriously the admonishment in Romans 14:23 when Paul speaks of doing things against your conscience or without faith. A pure heart before God should be your priority as a leader. Many put affable conformity for the sake of job or position security as their main priority. I would caution greatly against this with this scripture as just one of many references.

"How do I know if I am failing? Nothing seems to be going the way I planned or envisioned it."

The encouraging aspect I have found in ministry-building (and sometimes rebuilding) is that there really is no such thing as "failure" as long as you remain humble and flexible. Being receptive to input from others sharing the condition of one's heart with close confidants will be instrumental in fighting Satan's attacks of discouragement and defeat. Being flexible is necessary and essential. Things do not always go the way we plan, but keep in mind that the ways of God are infinite and can ultimately take you places you never thought you could go. I am always encouraged by Isaiah 55:8-9 in the Old Testament. God spells out that His thoughts, ways and ideas are much higher than ours. Be flexible, faithful and patient as God reveals His own plans using those creative and proactive energies He has already placed in our hearts and actions. I have, over the years, come to learn that ministry (no matter the size or focus) should be viewed as organic and pliable and evolve as a minister himself evolves as a leader and strategist. Ultimate failure (in oversimplified terms) comes when a leader resists being flexible regarding the different directions in which God might be taking the ministry. When a leader becomes obstinate and unmovable in his ideas, the ministry becomes stagnant under his leadership and actually begins to deteriorate. A stern warning to keep our hearts accountable as leaders can be found in Jeremiah 23:1-3 when God warns those who would consider themselves shepherds of His people. Focus on selfish ambition and a heart turned obstinate will yield very destructive fruit indeed. To reiterate my earlier point, God is more interested in the condition of one's heart during the journey. The end goal is just a vehicle that initiates the journey. Both are important but have different purposes in refining one as a leader.

"How do I introduce new ideas and cultivate new dynamics in my ministry"?

By now it should be clear that good working relationships are essential for building a ministry. These will present great opportunities to "play" with different ideas about how to improve one's current ministry situation. A leader who builds consensus among his confidants will accomplish several things. He will build excitement by revealing the potential for change and growth, strengthen current relationships by thinking through the possibilities, and cultivate new relationships by exploring the widest possible range of ideas. Through this process, such a leader will tap the potential of the broadest possible pool of talent. It is amazing that all this growth can come simply from brainstorming ways to infuse new ideas!

"Is my ministry salvageable"?

My earlier concept of "simplicity" will help one determine whether or not his ministry is salvageable. If a ministry's mission can be broken down into a basic vision, concept or idea, one will find that changing the process by which he carries out the mission will not be as difficult as he had imagined. For example, if benevolence is the goal of a ministry and one makes a goal of raising $1 million to donate to a given charity, he has formulated an admirable goal indeed. Biblical text supports this type of endeavor completely. As the ministry begins to plan the capital campaign, a sense of excitement and synergy will develop. However, one might want to reconsider the monetary amount of the goal if the ministry has only ten members who are involved in fundraising and the timeline for raising the money is only a month. The solution to such a dilemma is not to scrap the fundraising ministry but to revise the goal! Every ministry has the possibility of survival if the overall concept lines up consistently with biblical values and the leadership is unified with God, His spirit and His Word.

"I have no idea what I am doing. Can someone help me?"

Buy this book, read its content, and apply its concepts!

"I was given a ministry to care for, and my oversight pastor and I don't really know where to go from here. How do we find help when we need it?"

Buy two of my books…one for each of you!

CHAPTER 8

What are we really trying to accomplish?

Everyone has his or her own vision and agenda, so that the mission and priorities become confused. How do we get everyone in "agreement" as we go forward in growing our ministry?

As a leader one must decide on a standard or spiritual "axis" around which all aspects of his ministry will revolve. As simple as this might sound, I have noticed that many of the churches I have visited, worked in or consulted do not use the Bible as the accepted standard of God! If there is a lack of consensus that the Word of God is the ABSOLUTE standard of every facet and level of one's ministry, very little in this book will help him or his ministry.

Compromise without Biblical justifications can further cloud and/ or dilute the original vision.

Unfortunately, some men and women who are leading churches and subordinate ministries operate according to standards based on personal philosophies, traditions and methodologies, as well as a hodgepodge of other personal beliefs and references. Many Christians, and especially leaders, are very strong in their personal opinions about how to handle spiritual issues. Although some aspects of a leader's philosophy might be based loosely on the Bible, so many true Christian leaders lack the biblical knowledge to discern which beliefs are heretical. The conviction to fight Biblical distortions and inappropriate applications of the Word that the perpetrators of heresy often engage in goes unchallenged. It is essential that a specific church and its subordinate ministries agrees from the beginning that the Bible will be the standard and common "language" or vernacular as I have commonly referred to it in this writing, spoken by ALL involved in its ministries—from new convert to experienced leader. Everything must "line up" biblically—or at least not run contrary to biblical teachings.

"How did we (I) get so overwhelmed? When and how did things get so complicated?"

Things can get very complicated very quickly when a disciplined adherence to simplicity in the above-mentioned areas is not given its due diligence and attention. Everything in life can become very complicated when a ministry disregards discipline, planning and adherence to the master plan. Ministry complications can add up more rapidly than most problems one has in life because more people are involved in the process.

Many ministries experience the age-old problem of "bottlenecking." What is "bottlenecking?"

Too many leaders are so caught up in the daily details and the minutiae of their ministry work that they forget to teach what they are learning to someone whose help they will need as the ministry's work becomes more demanding. Many leaders actually do not want to share their authority with others because of ego and paranoia of sorts. Many other leaders of a similar personality type tend to gravitate toward the age-old pyramid model of leadership. This model of leadership helps to ensure that the primary leader always remains the focal point of leadership and authority. This is a very dangerous dynamic I see much too often in God's church. Some call this dynamic "building a crystal cathedral" around oneself in order to control all aspects of a rapidly-growing ministry. Others refer to this condition as "empire building". Both are deadly, and I would caution anyone who encounters a leader who shows these tendencies to look out for cultish propensities, which I will discuss later in more detail. When a leadership group or team does not grow numerically or in maturity in conjunction with the ministry in-question, this is commonly referred to as a "bottleneck". If a leader's goal is to grow the ministry he leads, he must be willing to share his leadership responsibilities as well as his/ her authority. A leader must be assertive and proactive in growing his/ her leadership group in faithful anticipation of an overall growth and need of the ministry as a whole. In order to ensure future sustainability as the ministry expands, a leader must train and prepare others to share the work as the ministry's commitments increase. In the book of Exodus chapter 18, after seeing how Moses set himself up as sole leader of God's remnant, Moses' father in law, Jethro, told Moses that what he was doing was "not good" (Exodus 18:17). Jethro advised Moses to delegate leadership responsibilities to trustworthy men to carry out as they themselves served God's people in smaller numeric divisions. This expedited the process of teaching and enforcing God's law in a more organized and expeditious way thereby making Moses' own governorship more frugal and effective.

What we have "built on" has come back to haunt us.

Without a disciplined or strategic approach such as that discussed in this book, then chaos will be the inevitable outcome. In a worst-case-scenario, but not uncommon or unheard-of, many churches and subordinate ministries have gone on for so long with very little structure, direction, discipline and leadership that what is now left seems absolutely chaotic and unmanageable.

In several case scenarios there may be a gross lack of leadership to lead the number of people in your ministry causing it to bog down. In other situations, there may be no cohesion, adherence to biblical orthodoxy in message, vision or "vernacular" causing mass disunity and structural unrest. In some situations, there may be too much of everything: rules, structure, mission, dogma…giving way to a rigid and inorganic legalism totally choking out God's Holy Spirit all together. Sometimes when a ministry is struggling, leadership, or a replacement leadership team, will go to the extreme of trying to "fix" the situation by putting a chokehold on everything with strict, overbearing and "micro-managing" mandates, rules and/ or protocols.

Keeping things simple is a very important discipline.

So many ideas, voices, distractions, and so forth can emerge as a ministry grows and evolves that it can become difficult for a leader or leaders to keep everything proceeding in an orderly fashion. I will emphasize once again that a ministry leader can "keep the door open" on all the different synergistic elements indicative of a healthy thriving ministry even while staying loyal and unwavering in her adherence to those simple "axis/ lynchpin" concepts that I discussed earlier. Keep that original goal or vision simple; stick to it; and enforce it lovingly and gently. A leader who does these things will find the daily processes involved in maintaining and perpetuating his ministry to be more manageable. In a thriving ministry, many people will want to have input into the ongoing process of evolving the ministry. Not every idea has to be implemented to make people feel useful and respected. What people seem to want most is to at least have their input considered and taken seriously. A thoughtful and insightful leader will take heed of all the creative and synergistic input he/ she receives gratefully, receptively and sincerely. In some cases where someone might be passionate about their idea or input, if unusable or non-pertinent at the time, at least give timely feedback and encourage more proactive involvement of that group or individual. As a leader, you can manage and perpetuate the ongoing quest for streamline simplicity regarding your ministry overall. Considering the many ideas and thoughts from your members, though they can sometimes have a tendency to make things more complicated, should be treated very respectfully and sincerely whether you are considering the input or not. People will take more ownership of their ministry when they feel that their voice is important. Be determined to keep your ministry simple while balancing the different creative energies your members want to bring.

CHAPTER 9

What Is Your Personal/ Group Doctrinal Foundation?

Bible

The Bible is multifaceted and contains fundamental teachings, character examples, life parallels, and so forth. It is complete in and of itself and needs no help from outside sources to complete its meaning. In 2 Timothy 3:16-17, we see that God's Word is complete and relevant in dealing with every facet of our lives. Though what I just wrote seems very obvious and oversimplified, I wrote it for a reason. Many people do not believe, whether by word or action, that the Bible is complete in and of itself. Many want other sources of spirituality to be encompassed into their daily ministry "vernacular". Be strong and unyielding in keeping the Bible as the ultimate authority and standard by which to live and lead.

Luck

Lack of planning, structure and discipline is a recipe for certain failure. Many with good hearts and noble intentions fall into the trap of relying on chance, happenstance, serendipity, and their ability to generate momentum. Some even go a step farther in this "rabbits foot/ four leaf clover"- type of leading by considering it "faith! Blind optimism is not faith, nor is it a substitute for it.

Philosophy

Some base their doctrinal beliefs on a hybrid mix of the Bible, therapy, psychology, myth, hearsay, rumor, traditional stories and imagination. A philosophy thus formulated is a recipe for heresy.

Dogma

Many ministers are not lacking in charisma (i.e., King Saul in the Old Testament). They project the force of their personality in order to stage an emotional drama that amplifies their peculiar theological and philosophical recipe punctuated by verbal extravagances . For example, forms of hyper-emotional or "ecstatic" worship atmospheres rely heavily upon a strong sense of emotion and "mysticism" to both validate and propagate an aura of "God's presence".

Democracy

Some leaders or ministries do not have a central figure making the judgment calls. They rely on a group or board consensus to make decisions. This can actually be very productive and fruitful if done correctly, but it can be very destructive if the scriptures are not the foundation of all consensus-based decision-making. Democracy is important but can also be subjective, capricious, and stray away from a Biblical basis depending on the pervading culture of the ministry in question. Sometimes, on the corporate level, a smaller group within the larger decision-making body is more effective in making the final call concerning matters of judgment for a specific situation of pertinence. The key to success will be flexibility and a willingness to let the subordinate ministries have more ownership of their own agendas.

"Winging it"

Some ministries start out and survive without any central focus, discipline or biblically-based mechanisms in place for teaching and advising mechanisms. Being flexible and open –minded is not "winging it" as some like to intertwine the two concepts. Incoherence is a recipe for disaster, as it usually leads to unwieldiness, dissention, and discouragement for all involved. The end result is typically a total abandonment of the ministry. This is a most regretful outcome. I have seen the tendency to "wing it" ultimately wipe out vital small-group ministries. Mindful planning, implementation and execution should be a concern and conviction for any ministry wanting to grow.

Gobbledygook

Much like the practice of "winging-it", philosophical incoherence can cause a ministry to fail. Many ministry leaders start with a noble vision but find it difficult to lay a solid spiritual foundation and develop the practical mechanisms necessary to sustain strong and consistent growth. A loose concatenation of ideas and mantras does not contribute to philosophical coherence or support an orderly operating procedure. It becomes very difficult for a leader to rally his membership around a gumbo of unstable philosophical fragments bonded together in a montage. Incoherence tends to be a problem mostly, though not exclusively, for local small group ministries. Having a robust diversity of thought and ideas is not only important for any ministry, but essential. A leader must implement a base or foundation of biblical principles that will serve as a reference or guide by which all actions and ideas can be measured and held accountable.

CHAPTER 10

What Are You Willing to Change to Achieve Ministry Goals?

"Ego"-the silent "ministry killer".

Is ego driving the desire to lead? Ego-gratification might be the underlying motive for leading a ministry if a person is interested in presiding over only a large and/ or extremely visible corporate group, if he is possessive about ministry responsibilities and insecure delegating assignments to other qualified members, and if he believes that the ministry's public image must be based on him. Ego is also an issue if a leader rejects helpful feedback or holds at a distance those with qualified backgrounds in ministry that can offer very constructive input. These traits usually stem from feelings of personal insecurity or paranoid apprehensions toward potential allies. Many leaders, as "empire builders", have a sinful propensity to be covetous and protective of their own leadership image . I will cite King Saul as a major example of this. It was obvious to most Jews that David was a talented general and warrior who helped Saul win many wars, yet instead of being grateful and giving David more responsibility, Saul looked to hold David back and ultimately kill him. Saul was so insecure about David's popularity and success that he tried to have David killed! This kind of paranoid behavior is a significant concern and can result in a contentious relationship with God for both the leader in question and his/ her ministry. I have seen leaders allow someone to "shine" when the situation calls for it but interject something in reference to how the success of that particular person is tied to the primary leader's "vision" for this person's success. I usually refer to this dynamic as self-proclaimed "proxy" or "piggybacking". A leader will use someone else's success to emphasize their own personal involvement and bearing on that success.

If a leader's ultimate goal is protecting the condition of his own heart before God, he must be honest in assessing the role of self-glorification in his motives.

Allow council/ advice

If a ministry leader is unwilling to seek advice from members known to have wisdom and expertise, and if he is uncomfortable letting others know he does not have all the answers, that leader has a serious problem to address before sustainable growth can occur. Many ministries become derailed by leaders who will seek feedback only from those who will flatter them. I think of 2 Timothy 4:3 in this situation. Leaders insulate themselves with "trusted advisors" made up of over- agreeable men and women who are usually very intelligent but more concerned with finding acceptance and affirmation by giving flattery-based input and feedback.

You must be willing to admit that something must change.

Do not be afraid of what people will think if you are flexible and humble. Do not be afraid to admit mistakes and relinquish some "control". "Control freaks" whose sense of security is grounded in their authoritative power over the corporate body or small-group ministry can ultimately undermine one of them or both. I think of the book of 3 John when John is encouraging his friend Gaius to take heart that help will come. The church leader at that point, Diotrephes, was rejecting the saints being sent by the apostle John to encourage the church and help. The believers in the church there were beginning to be stressed by Diotrephes' lack of willingness to embrace the help being sent. This is how we can tend to make the people in our ministry feel when we as leaders are not willing to get the help we need, or at least being offered, when things have become very challenging.

Do not be afraid to step out of your comfort zone.

A strong leader is willing to change direction, seek and implement advice, and be flexible with his plans and vision. He is willing to take a lesser role for the greater good, the bigger picture, and the future of his ministry. A spiritual leader with God and his ministry first in his heart will see himself as a facilitator rather than an "overlord" or taskmaster. As obvious as all of this sounds, the reality is incredibly concerning to say the least regarding the common practice of ministers setting themselves up to be overlords and taskmasters rather than servants and facilitators.

A faithful leader allows others to challenge him.

A confident leader surrounds himself with people who are honest and empowered to speak their mind as needed, and he appreciates when they do. He seeks people who can challenge him and holds himself to a standard of accountability that has nothing to do with sycophancy. A secure leader does not have to be coddled. His self-regard is not tied to accolades and adoration; it is tied to service for God. A respected leader is considered a peer rather than a patriarch in his discipleship group; he views leadership as a truly plural concept and a team effort rather than as a hierarchy. A devout leader is humble before his human limitations. He invests more energy in fulfilling the ministry's mission than in compensating for his insecurities and shortcomings. The worst thing that can happen in a ministry is to be headed by a leader who believes his position or title places him above all others and elevates him beyond reproach. Drastic spiritual measures must be taken to remedy any situation in which someone in a compromised spiritual state is leading a ministry.

Take calculated risks to shake things up.

A wise leader is willing to change what is not working and to experience the discomfort of failure. He is willing to let someone else take a greater role in something he is passionate about even if that person shows a greater potential for success in that particular area. He is willing to be known for being flexible and giving others a chance to have more significant input in the building process rather than for being rigid. He does not need the ministry's successes to appear to have emanated from him.

CHAPTER 11

Protocols and Traditions

Are you truly allowing for growth?

If there is a system in place for carrying out certain tasks or handling certain situations, is it flexible enough to accommodate growth and change? Traditions and protocols need to be effective in accomplishing a ministry leader's personal goals and the ministry's collective goals. A leader's personal shortcomings should not limit the ministry. He should consider analyzing the ministry's plans and strategies to be part of his routine responsibilities. He should know and understand his leadership style and keep the strengths and weaknesses of that style in mind as he trains and cultivates subordinate leaders. He should be willing to go to any lengths sanctioned in the eyes of God to see his ministry succeed. He should be willing to appoint someone else as a leader, assistant, or mentor if doing so meant greater growth and advancement for that specific ministry. These are very high standards, but a person should not aspire to a position of leadership if he is unwilling to assess himself honestly according to them.

Are you truly inclusive?

A ministry leader's members should feel confident that he is in a position to grow the ministry and sincerely seek ways to bring others in. His membership should feel that his highest priority is carrying out the ministry's mission—not that his whims are the primary catalyst for the ministry's activity and structure.

Are you truly flexible?

A sound ministry has room for growth. There should be room for evaluation and possible change in direction or protocol if the intended results are either not forthcoming or improbable. Others should feel free to offer input and even to (respectfully) criticize the status quo, especially if that input can ultimately lead to positive change. A sound ministry should devote itself to serving others, not to serving self. I am inspired and convicted by Isaiah 55: 8-9 when God reminds us how much higher and greater His thoughts and ways are than ours. In knowing this and always keeping this in mind when "things don't go our way" as leaders, stay confident that God may be taking you and your ministry in several different and potentially very fruitful directions. Our will must always be subordinate to God's will for our ministries.

CHAPTER 12

How does this all work?

Creating a common language so that we can all communicate in a "common" way within our church and ministries.

Most ministries start small and very easy to sustain. Many, as they begin to grow, become subject to the differing methods and ideas that come with the diverse people who become a part of that ministry via transfer or conversion. Because of the multiplicity of thoughts and approaches regarding what ministry leaders and members bring to the situation, a new dynamic begins to emerge. Very soon, communication starts to break down, and people are "all over the map" in their objectives, with no cohesive bond, because of a lack of foundation-building fundamentals. Communication erodes at a geometric rate as the ministry grows—first on the local level, then on the intermediate levels, and finally on the corporate level. The corporate group is now ripe for implosion regardless of its recent successes in achieving ministry goals.

How do we build ministry cohesiveness on local and corporate levels?

Though ministries may differ from one another in the specific groups they serve, and though they may differ in their goals and visions, fundamental commonalities built into the primary infrastructure of the ministry or ministries will ensure success in key areas of long-term sustainability and diversification.

Several of these "key" areas should include: communication, mission/ goals, social/ fellowship infrastructures, etc.

How do we establish proprietary and systematic coherency and homogeny?

Using the Bible as a foundational tool in as many areas as possible will ensure that a ministry's mission statement can be used as a rallying point as a ministry's group dynamics become more complex. Maintaining multiple ministries is easy when leaders plan thoughtfully about a universal communication strategy that ties everything together so that the outcome is not one church or ministry that looks like a number of different "little churches or ministries" going in different directions. The desired effect should be one church with a number of richly diverse ministries all supporting a central theme and mission. Everything in essence becomes a vehicle by which different people with different needs can all meet at a central intersection that serves as the "head of the spear," as Nelson Mandela would call it. Umkhonto we Sizwe—"tip of the spear"—was the name and rallying call of Nelson Mandela's underground leadership group the African National Congress during the turbulent years of popular resistance to apartheid in South Africa. Mandela spent many years in hiding but was eventually discovered and imprisoned. While incarcerated, he continued to lead the civil rebellion with amazing effectiveness because the ANC's core mission continued to be the guiding force. Similarly, a church and its ministries should formulate a clear mission, decide upon a strategy for implementing it, and stay that course without wavering. For instance, if a large corporate church claims that its mission is to "love people" yet has an overactive, a la carte agenda that requires many groups, classes and ministries to carry it out, it can appear exclusive or cliquey to outside observers, especially if it has a stagnant fellowship and a lack of depth and dynamism. The mission and message become confused and diluted; consequently, disagreement and discouragement will eventually cause a breakdown somewhere. People will simply defect to other churches. Unfortunately, defection has become quite the norm in today's church culture. Unfortunately, this is why many churches and subordinate ministries tend to focus more on "showy" worship services and "over-busy" Sunday school-type class activities rather than ways to grow more intimacy, family and unity within the overall fellowship corporately and locally.

CHAPTER 13

Benefits of Biblical Ministry Efficiency

The following points represent ideal benefits of simplifying and condensing your ministry structures.

- Simplifying enables a church to develop a consistent and fluid approach to managing both single and multiple ministries.
- It provides more efficient use of leadership
- It also provides a more efficient use of communication from leadership to congregation trickling down from the large, corporate level to the local, small-group levels.
- It maximizes leadership's ability to review ministry activity at all levels in order to evaluate it for effectiveness and efficiency.

The following points represent some possible (very simple) biblical principles to build your ministry around regardless of its size. The process whereby a church attains these goals can potentially open the door to many creative thoughts and ideas. In other words, "fleshing out" the plans to achieve biblically simple goals will be the joy of the journey. Remember: these are just a few examples.

- Streamline and simplify the vision
- Seek and save the lost; make disciples; develop an evangelistic culture
- Grow the ministry in Biblical knowledge of God. Grow in daily, pragmatic and applicable knowledge of the Bible.
- Maintain, protect and support the maturation of the saved within the ministry.
- Be flexible and creative. A leader can stay focused on his vision if it is simple and attainable. Never be afraid to be flexible in the face of uncertain factors. How one fleshes out his strategy for attaining key goals keeps ministry fun and interesting for people.

CHAPTER 14

Setting Goals

Evaluate

If plans for a given ministry have not yielded the desired results, or if the ministry is not meeting important benchmarks within a reasonable time frame, it could be that the ministry's goals are unrealistic. Factors such as size of a church's ministries, their growth rate, the growth rate for leaders, conversions, visitors, diversification of ministries and so on should all be aligned with a church's specific situation, evaluated conservatively. Failure to attain goals can be discouraging for a ministry. The easiest way to avoid this result is to set conservative goals. How a ministry leader sets goals and his approach to achieving them can reveal a lot about a leader's strengths and weaknesses.

Never fear change when goal-setting.

When goals seem to be unattainable within a finite and reasonable period, it might be time to re-evaluate either the goal or the timeline. Different goals will have different timelines and will require different conditions of possibility for their success. When a ministry keeps its goals simple and few, the chances for success and general satisfaction increase. However, if goals feel unattainable and a pervading sense of discouragement has set in, it might be time to assess and revise. For example, sometimes the person formulating the goals and devising the strategies for their attainment is not the best person for that particular job. If ministry members work as a team whose first priority is to glorify God, there will be little room for one individual to jeopardize the entire ministry by pushing his own agenda, thereby threatening the condition of his own heart.

Trust the Spirit of God when setting goals.

Ultimately, the growth of a ministry is up to God. Leaving things up to God and his spirit, though, is never an excuse to plan poorly or fail to plan altogether. Too many ministries and their leaders rely too much on personal talents, dogma, luck, blind optimism, and the like and rationalize incompetence and obstinate inexperience as "relying on the spirit". As in any area of life, discipline in ministry will determine success at some significant level .Proverbs 14:23 is a very good and practical scripture to set our mind when setting and achieving goals. Hard work in planning, implementing and executing any set of plans will take a great deal of wisdom, discipline and maturity. One cannot get by with just mere talk and compulsion.

As well, prayer and study of the Word should not only be a part of the planning, implementation and execution of a ministry's growth strategy, but should also be the ministry's foundation with all aspects of the system tied directly to Biblical text and the ideas construed from that text conceptually explicit and implicit.

Never be afraid to face hard truths when dealing with yourself and your ministry.

A leader must be willing to evaluate himself honestly with the ministry's best interest in mind. He must ask, "Did I plan well or appropriately?" "Am I the right person to set goals and devise strategy?" "What do others think about how I carried out my role?" "Am I flexible enough to change my role in order to allow the ministry to flourish, or am I set in what I do, ultimately putting myself above the needs of the ministry?"

CHAPTER 15

Goals

How do I set long-term goals?

A ministry's short-term goals should feed directly into its long-term goals. With this being the case, a ministry leader must have some idea of where his sees his ministry in five, ten, or even fifteen to twenty years. He must remain steadfast in keeping the ministry on a direct path to those goals, have the support of top-tier leadership, and help to create a culture of support within the entire corporate body. Sometimes a local or small-group ministry can exceed the vision and limits of the corporate body. When a small-group ministry grows rapidly and exponentially, it becomes necessary to create stronger spiritual bonds among its members. This might be achieved by conducting Bible study in a way that makes for stronger conversions, modifying relationship protocols in order to make male and female ministries more distinct and independent, and demanding a high level of maturity in cooperative communication.

How do I set short term goals?

A short-term goal is one that is achievable within six months to two years. However, the process of formulating, planning, and implementing short-term goals differs little from formulating, planning, and implementing long-term goals. In order for short-term goals to be successful, one must stay on a consistent course and calibrate the method and pace toward attaining those goals in a way that will allow for regular assessment, input from others, and if necessary, revision.

It is best to be flexible with goals. Often the process involved in attaining the goals one has set will result in a re-evaluation of those goals instead of a formulation of new ones. In order for a ministry to bear fruit, those involved in it must be flexible and humble enough to accept a possible shift in course.

Something to keep in mind is that many great inventions of the modern day such as radios, televisions, telephones, lights, and the like were perfected through trial and error and flexibility. Although the original concept was the product of one inventor's imagination and ingenuity, the invention evolved as others gave their input until the invention's overall design became what it is today. It is very important to note in goal setting that facilitating an atmosphere of excitement , creativity and proactive participation in the goal-setting process will yield a greater sense of ownership and loyalty to the goal by your collective ministry. Get as many people as involved as possible sensibly, creatively and proactively. Most people have a hard time supporting a goal thought up by one or two people. People also have a hard time supporting a goal made by few individuals they do not believe confidently relate to what the needs may be en masse. God may have put a goal on the heart of the leader or leaders to explore, but a wise leader will consult many advisors and listen to what is being said before deciding on a course of action. Proverbs 15:22 is a great example of God's attitude for any leader regarding his/ her plans. The difference between success and failure could be determined by how aggressively you seek the council, wisdom and advice of other.

CHAPTER 16

The Concept of Biblical Discipleship is Universal

Every ministry in a church must speak the same "language" or vernacular as I like to refer to it. Using different curricula, teaching materials and Bible supplements creates a cumbersome and thus unsustainable teaching dynamic. Multiple curricula and supplements can create a communication divide between ministries. An incoherent message compromises a ministry's ability to create an organic learning environment in which rank and file members can learn and be stimulated alongside the new visitor who is there for the first time. In an atmosphere in which everyone seems to interpret scripture based on his or her own experiences, the choices can be overwhelming. I would caution a ministry leader not to get caught up in the latest curricular fads being promoted by celebrity "ministers". Relying heavily on pre-written curricula hampers a leader's ability to study and teach the Bible creatively and authentically. Pre-written curricula are all about giving "answers" regarding scripture but not teaching "process".

I would advise a ministry leader not to make celebrity ministers rich by buying their books, but to make the members of his ministry rich in knowledge by teaching them to interface intimately with scripture, thereby empowering them to do the same with others.

Each ministry should be different only in personality.

The only difference between ministries should be the individual personalities of the group. Tailoring one's teaching and motivational style to the specific needs of the group will help to create coherence and build synergy. Supplemental curricula may be used on special occasions, but doing so should be an exception and not a rule. The Bible should be the primary text and the foundation for ministry curricula. Holding oneself to a high standard of discipline in that regard creates a universal template for leadership. The Bible is a great curriculum and common denominator for teaching. I would advise ministry leaders to enjoy the inherent simplicity of God's Word, especially in the Gospels, because there will be more than enough complexities to keep him or her busy without creating more.

Build effective and efficient ministry principles into the foundation of your church or ministry.

A ministry should be "organic", meaning that it is run in a way that guiding principles and goals can evolve naturally over time. Building around simple goals grounded in scripture will allow for greater flexibility regarding pending shifts and changes. Keeping the initial goals that you set basic will allow a ministry to streamline the more complicated facets of its daily operations. The more aspects that a leader can keep simple and efficient, the easier it will be to maintain the cohesiveness of a ministry even as it grows.

Keep things simple can be more difficult than one may guess.

Simple ministry principles and structure allow for greater growth with fewer complexities. The most effective philosophy for any activity is to keep things like infrastructure, programming and lesson material basic. Simplicity within key components of a ministry allows a leader to add depth and difficulty as needed. For example, using the Bible as the primary text for a lesson simplifies teaching, but from it an individual leader can not only make a given lesson as deep or challenging as is appropriate for a specific group or occasion, but also develop a spiritual language that unifies the congregation. Be very aware of the propensity of many strong and creative leaders to have a tendency to make things more complicated than they should be. In a world of traditional religion and legalism, many believers tend to gravitate towards rigid structures, "ready-made" carricula, ingrained traditions, etc. Sometimes just keeping things simple can become very difficult and complicated because of the pride that comes with legalism and religious tradition. A good example of this behavior can be found throughout the Gospels regarding the actions of the Pharisees and Sadducees overcomplicating God's law. Jesus came to simplify the Message so that all would have the opportunity to follow Him. Take encouragement from Jesus in His own struggle to convince people of the gracefully and miraculously simple way God wishes to embrace His children. I would also admonish any leader or potential leader to take note of the actions of the religious ruling councils and how they fought to complicate this whole process.

Keep the Bible at the center of all things.

Churches that started with a membership of one hundred can be stable if the membership grows to one-thousand or beyond if its infrastructure is built with an aim toward developing and maintaining cohesion. If the Bible is the center of all teaching and the basis for all communication between ministries, congregants will be able to reap the benefit of this structural simplicity no matter how large the membership becomes. Simplicity also makes possible deeper discussion and analysis on a corporate level and consequently allows the message to trickle down to the local and small-group levels intact. Under these conditions, top-tier leadership can further its communiqué' on the local and small group levels: leadership can then break the message down level by level, with the result being that the entire organization "digests" corporate-level communication in role-specific ways.

CHAPTER 17

Plan Proactively to Grow Leaders

Exercise preemptive and proactive training of young and potential leaders. Train leaders with an aim toward preparing them for the many scenarios they will encounter in their specific duties or responsibilities as a leader. Many ministries release leaders into their specific field of responsibility with very little ministry-specific training. In many situations, the oversight leadership responsible for training are themselves ill equipped to train others comprehensively so that they will be equipped to handle any situation. Failure to train leaders properly can create a damaging situation that might require drastic ameliorative measures. When those in upper-tier leadership lack the skill and expertise to train subordinate leaders so that they can flourish in their ministry, the novices might feel that they are not being supported, become discouraged, and resign.

When subordinate ministers resign in significant numbers, they leave a destructive vacuum in a ministry. Consequently corporate ministry might scrap the idea of developing a much-needed and potentially vital ministry with the justification that "it just does not work" and is not productive. Small-group ministries are often jettisoned by way of this reasoning. To preserve them is one of the inspirations for the writing in this book. When small-group ministries become difficult to manage, larger corporate groups sometimes turn to a "Sunday school" approach to ministry-management and outreach while the "lead minister/ pastor" continues to lead the whole church as "one big bible talk/ small group". Though Sunday school paradigms have their place and usefulness, they are not an adequate or equivalent substitute for small-group ministries and the specific role they play within a corporate dynamic. Sunday school scenarios involve minimal intimate social interaction, and little if any planned or inherent group interaction. In regard to selecting and developing leaders, they require little except a willing volunteer with little or no expertise in that particular area with the simple expectation of reciting from an established curriculum written by some "Christian celebrity". Also, because Sunday school classes function autonomously from one another and therefore do not make it a priority to develop ways of communicating effectively across ministries, they make a poor substitute for small-group ministries. They are also poorly equipped to deal with the growth rate that most churches need in order to advance their evangelism. To conclude, Sunday school programs have a limited impact. They are somewhat two-dimensional in the larger scope of dynamic ministry development.

Plan and anticipate for growth and sub-division quickly.

Train new leaders aggressively. Being proactive in not only training but in prospecting for leaders in preparation of forecasted growth is essential for expanding ministry on all levels. Many ministries have a crisis-based philosophy regarding training protocols and get bogged down by bottlenecking due to the lack of leadership to take care of the growing ministry and trying to manage several crises at once. The norm, unfortunately, for training leaders is often to find someone to fill a sudden or unexpected vacuum left for any number of reasons. Many times there was no one assisting or prepared at all to take the lead in this given situation. Unfortunately, small-group ministries and worship teams are primary victims of this dynamic. Ironically, both of these ministries usually possess the greatest potential for growth. Many times, a lack of leadership is the main culprit in hindering any forward moving growth.

When designed effectively, the small group ministry is specifically built to facilitate an atmosphere of fellowship by encouraging and cultivating intimate relationships, simple Bible-based teaching, and gentle yet consistent accountability by and for each member. Continuing to develop your leadership team to grow with this dynamic is of great importance and should take priority. Small-group ministries also involve some form of evangelism that balances the internal focus with the external focus. Because of its visibility, the worship team will often generate more interest than small-group ministries. An experienced leader will take advantage of the internal strengths of both small-group and worship teams and find a proactive way to accommodate multilateral growth both in congregant membership as well as leadership with equal emphasis.. I took the time to mention worship team(s) here in this segment because I believe that a worship team can and should function like a small group. If the worship team ministry is too large, say 15 people or more, then you simply make two or more small groups out of that ministry and integrate them infrastructurally into the corporate body in the same way you would any other small group. In all circumstances, an experienced leader will have prepared leadership actively leading, training and assisting as well as being prospected for handling the growth forecasts as they materialize.

Never give up on believing in people!

Most Christians come into a ministry with a desire to do something in service for God. The experienced and mature leader of faith actively searches out people who have a desire to lead and creates opportunities for them to keep those fires of evangelism burning in their heart. Many Christians have this flame extinguished by leaders in ministries they join because the ministry leader's rigid adherence to tradition and protocol, together with his fear and insecurity, siphons the life and enthusiasm out of the ministry. Under the guise of training or pre-screening candidates for subordinate leadership, many leaders want people to wait or prove themselves. However, identifying people who have the potential and desire to serve the Lord is the responsibility of any effective leader should he want to grow his ministry proactively. Identifying ministry leaders who are secure, flexible, creative, and charismatic enough to find and develop other leaders in service of God's kingdom benefits the overall ministry. Christians waiting to be developed into leaders are usually very abundant, but ministries often lack top-tier leaders who are confident, secure and proactive enough to figure out creative ways to develop strong subordinate leaders. A mature and spiritual leader acts as a facilitator by creating opportunities for others to work and serve in ministry situations. Unfortunately, the norm seems to be that leaders create a hierarchy of leadership, perch at the top of the pyramid, and from that position delegate power to the same trusted few. Through the control they have over their trusties, these leaders preside over every aspect of the ministry as a taskmaster rather than as a servant for God.

Allow developing leaders to make their own mistakes

Empower new and potential leaders-in-training to make decisions within controlled parameters. Give them small responsibilities on a project and mentor them until the project is complete. The main goal with this method of training is not the result, but rather the process and how this process will affect their development in spiritual and logistical respects. Increase the trainees' responsibility as they grow in maturity, awareness and their ability to handle a variety of situations. As long as the trainee shows a determination to learn, do not be alarmed by his or her mistakes or missteps along the way. Mistakes and errors are often the best teacher.

Many leaders are reluctant to train people because they lack the skill, flexibility, and confidence to take a proactive disposition toward training new leaders. Because these leaders are perceived as a threat, people who do show a great attitude and ethic toward ministry work, they block the chances of such "potential rivals" by politely ignoring them. Attitudes like this ultimately stymie the advancement of God's kingdom. It has been my opinion and personal conviction, and continues to be so, that a good leader/ trainer will "train himself out of a job". What I mean by this is that you must go into training someone with a great vision for God's Kingdom as a whole. Some of those you train may show a very distinct aptitude and carry with that the potential to serve in greater capacities than yourself. I look forward to being able to see those I train surpass me in the Lord's service! This, unfortunately, is not the general attitude of most trainers. Insecurity, competition and impure motives cannot be allowed to permeate the heart of those who have been entrusted to train and lead.

Be consistent in nurturing and giving proper consistent attention to those who are training.

A key component in training someone (which takes a great deal of patience, discipline and vision) is consistent nurturing. Communicating consistently and encouragingly to your trainee will expedite his/ her development and yield great long-term benefits. Many leaders fall into the trap of giving a new leader a commission or responsibility (usually out of great and sudden need or plain desperation) and do a poor job of specifying what will be expected of them, the goals of a particular project, and how the trainee will be supported. Failure to communicate clear expectations, to outline specific goals, and to devise a plan for a trainees' success and the success of the project are indicative of undisciplined, unspiritual and/ or inexperienced oversight leadership.

One of the focuses of a leader's ministry is the development and success of those whom he is entrusted to train. Giving someone a new responsibility or project is only the first step in the long, concentrated process of building a culture of strong leadership. Another point to remember is that, although a given leader might have an established training method that has proven to be effective, each person is different and therefore motivated by different things. A leader would be wise to tailor his training strategies to each individual. I will again refer to this dynamic as "organic" in one's approach to ministry and in this training-specific situation. However universal and biblically sound one's vision and strategy may be, it is smart to build flexibility into the training strategy so that each trainee may develop his or her own style. Holding the space for others to explore their leadership potential is essential to the process of creating that "organic" and synergistic atmosphere in which joyful, motivated and creative leaders—leaders who will ultimately be able to support the ministry's goals—may thrive.

On the local and small-group levels of a corporate entity, individuality can and should be encouraged, in contrast to the overweening push towards quiet submission and conformity, in order to achieve ministry goals and make the overall vision a reality. If, for example, a church's vision is to have a greater evangelistic impact on a certain area of the city, and the Bible sets the ministry's moral and procedural standard and drives its own local curriculum as a proprietary learning base, a strong leader will encourage each subordinate to bring his/ her own personality and strengths to bear upon the achievement of that goal. The responsibility of upper-tier leadership is to set goals and establish parameters within which those goals can be achieved, but which also allow individual leaders a degree of autonomy and creative freedom. Oversimplifying my point in conclusion of this segment; we are her to facilitate the growth and maturity of individual, energetic and synergistic leaders. We are not here to create over agreeable robots and mindless conformist which I have seen in many situations over my years and experiences.

Chapter 18

Plan Proactively and Assertively to Grow Small Groups

How do we think about and develop small group evangelism?

Evangelistic strategies can vary as much as a ministry's imagination will allow. Each group will want to meet and invite people in a way unique to their group makeup and target goals. At this small-group, local level, evangelism can be a joyful and energizing part of a ministry's lifestyle. Evangelism is not only a mission from Jesus as we see in Matthew 28:18-20 where Jesus gives us His last words and evangelistic mission in the Great Commission, but a way to further understand more about God as we see in Philemon 1:6 where the bible speaks of having a greater understanding of God by actively sharing our faith. Sharing an evangelistic lifestyle is also a way to sustain the spiritual fervor, mission focus, and feeling of conquest in advancing God's kingdom through a church or specific ministry. Something to keep in mind is that evangelism should never be seen as an activity separate from what we already do as Christians or how we live our lives. Evangelism should be considered (as it is taught by a leader who lives this himself) an integral part of our lives. It should be intertwined and with every activity we participate in and our every interaction with others. Church/ministry leaders should set a high standard of evangelism for all who consider themselves true believers of God. Evangelism is not an issue of ability or gifting, as some would like to think; rather, all God's people are called to evangelism, as it is a matter of faith, giving and love as I mentioned previously referencing the passage in Matthew 28:18-20.

If every ministry has this vibrancy and zeal as a byproduct of a well-focused and active group, the atmosphere of the larger corporate body will in turn reflect this level of excitement. A saying I heard as a young Christian sums up this principle perfectly: "How the small group goes is how goes the church" regarding many of the general and specific ministry dynamics mentioned in this writing. I would like to mention as a special note that when I speak of evangelism I am speaking of sharing your faith with those who would and could be considered a non-believer in God. There are many ways, which I will go into later in this writing, of sharing your faith. No "one way" of sharing God with someone is the absolute "only" way. Many different people, times, circumstances and reasons will warrant a litany of differing "if then" scenario resolutions (if I may borrow this antiquated syntax blurb to punctuate my point). I would like to emphasize that I do not believe that convincing other "believers" that one church is better, more attractive or a must to visit. This would not or should not be considered evangelism. Looking at the life and ministry of Jesus, especially through the Gospels, there are no examples of Jesus pitting one set of His followers in some sort of "presentation competition" against another. Inviting someone to your church knowing that they have a church of their own would be polite and socially courteous, but not what Philemon 1:6 was speaking of in terms of "actively sharing your faith". I make this last point of this segment because there is a serious confusion in the "Christian religious" community as to what evangelism is. Too many churches and specific ministries are more focused on trying to be the "flavor of the month" ministry simply inviting believers from other ministries to simply consider changing the address of their place of worship rather than looking for people specifically who are searching for God. Churches and smaller specific ministries who get caught up in the "revolving door" dynamic of believers simply going from church to church and ministry to ministry in an effort to boost attendance numbers are in great error regarding true evangelism. Be leery of such places.

What role does accountability play in small group ministry?

Accountability is another essential component of a successful evangelistic small group or local-level ministry. Keeping evangelism at the forefront of conversation is essential to unifying everyone behind the larger mission. Such an intense focus on evangelism can be intimidating for some. However, a wise leader will take into consideration the maturity level of each individual's faith when keeping people accountable. He should assume that if no one is talking about the mission to evangelize (as well as other key spiritual principles), the congregants are probably not giving these areas their due attention. An apt illustration of how easily it is to get off track when a leader fails to keep his people focused is the episode where Jesus reinstates his disciples after his resurrection. The twelve apostles walked with Jesus for over three years, yet in absence of His direct guidance, they had to be reminded of their mandate. Let me make this point of clarity and explanation. When I speak of accountability, I am NOT speaking of a harsh "big brother is looking down on you" or some "Orwellian" form of overbearing surveillance. This is not even Godly. I am simply speaking of having the discipline and courage to keep important issues in the forefront of conversation on all levels, whether individually or corporately, that would both challenge and edify others in your immediate vicinity of fellowship and ministry. For instance: if a brother is struggling with a certain issue and he has confided in you, do not be afraid to ask him how things are going with that "certain" issue as you offer friendship and prayer to him. This can hold true in plurality as well on all levels of ministry. As a leader, always exercise great tact, sensitivity and wisdom balanced with courage, concern and care.

Consistency is a powerful "calling card" for any leader or potential leader.

As I have mentioned above, the most critical component of any successful ministry endeavor is consistency. A strong leader builds his self-confidence and the confidence that others have in him through consistency and diligence. People feel they can trust and rely on someone who lives a lifestyle that conforms to the standards he sets for his flock. Consistency is a very important discipline which must be developed with time and maturity. For so many leaders regardless of specific responsibility, the only thing consistent in their life is "inconsistency". Making life, relationships and ministry much too complicated for any number of reasons can and will erode most any attempt at consistency. A resounding theme I will continue to "trumpet" throughout this writing is "keep things streamline and simple". Such is a direct path to a greater degree of discipline and, more specifically, consistency. A scripture from God's Word has served as a great reminder to me for many years in Ecclesiastes 7:18-"Whoever fears God will avoid all extremes". Finding a balance of all facets of your life will lead to an ongoing development of consistency in your life that will inspire your ministry to have a greater confidence in your leadership.

Creating a vision for yourself and your ministry is essential for long term development and viability.

A good leader has a vision and set goals for the ministry, but encourages individuals to establish goals for themselves as well. He finds out what each person's vision is and gently holds him or her accountable to that vision. He realizes that making or mandating goals for individuals can sometimes be counterproductive, so he leads by giving individuals the freedom to think and act as leaders for themselves. Creating a culture of leadership and accountability fosters each individual's sense of ownership of the collective ministry and enables each member to mature as a Christian. A great example I heard years ago was that shepherds lead their sheep not from the front where they can lose sight of stragglers, but from behind, "prodding" them gently with his voice and staff while keeping clear view of his flock and its surroundings.

CHAPTER 19

Anticipate Growth

Prospect for potential leadership in your ministry as if prospecting for gold!

Many times, as leaders, we get so caught up in the daily work of a ministry and its various distractions that we forget one of the most important aspects of being a ministry leader: identifying new leaders to train. Promising candidates can come from a number of different sources. Ideally, they will come from within the ministry. A person whom the ministry converted is most ideal since he/ she will have a thorough knowledge "from the ground up" about how the ministry works and what it expects from its members. Although it is human nature to prefer to work mostly—if not exclusively—with people whom one likes or connects with, choosing leaders based on personal preference is not always the best way to identify potential leaders. Too many leaders are chosen for their affability and "agreeability", which is often confused with loyalty. This method of choosing a leader, though comfortable in the short term, will have detrimental long-term effects on both the ministry and the leader responsible for training if it produces leaders who are likable but spiritually compromised or incompetent.

Identifying potential leaders who are agreeable is essential, but they should also have enough security in their own character and personality that they will not be apprehensive about speaking truthfully when challenges arise. I have witnessed many ministries begin auspiciously but weaken over time and ultimately fail because subordinate leaders feared speaking truthfully to the established oversight leadership. Sometimes subordinate leaders decline to speak their mind because top tier leaders have developed an aura of inapproachability or hold themselves above reproach. Leaders like this have injured many ministries. The members whom established leaders tap for leadership should be those with the greatest potential—observable by way of objective criteria—to secure the ministry's long-term viability. Only established leaders who are themselves spiritually sound are able to hold themselves to so high a standard of discipline that they are able to choose subordinate leaders who are best-qualified for a job, even if those individuals would not win a popularity contest. Showing wisdom in the selection of subordinate leadership is, ultimately, of the greatest importance. You can tell a lot about leaders by the people with whom they surround themselves. Ultimately, the potential success or failure of your ministry will depend largely on those you choose to train for leadership.

With whom are you sharing your faith?

In the same spirit of searching proactively for people within a ministry to train for potential leadership, a successful ministry leader will need to have a similar resolution about his/ her personal evangelism. He/ she will have to cultivate this passion for outreach in the people he leads. Ministries often fail to train leaders in the methods of evangelism so that the ministry can grow consistently. At the root of this failure is a lack of planning, foresight, maturity and emphasis.

Developing and nurturing relationships can be difficult if the leaders / trainers do not live a principled lifestyle centered upon a firm commitment to evangelism or other spiritual imperative that the ministry had deemed important. When ministry leaders do not have this principle as a part of their leadership and lifestyle, many in their respective churches and local ministries can be expected to exhibit the same deficiency. Many groups neglect cultivating evangelistic maturity as a fundamental component and merely suggest it in a sermon topic. This is a mistake. All the Gospels and written epistles emphasize the importance of evangelism. Leaving the responsibility to a public relations, outreach department, or specific ministry "willing" to do that work is not the model of the church put forward in the Bible.

Personal evangelism on the part of every ministry member lays the foundation for future relationships essential to the ministry's growth and sustainability. Evangelism is just as multifaceted as much as Jesus' ministry was. It might be inviting the checker at the grocery store to attend a Sunday sermon, giving a card to a sick friend, asking a schoolmate to come to a Bible study, or baking cookies for a neighbor. The idea is to create an opportunity to share "your life and doctrine" (1 Timothy 4:16). An experienced leader, and a fruitful one as well, learns to proselytize naturally and consistently, using almost every social opportunity life offers to extend an invitation (1 Cor. 9:19-23 NIV).

CHAPTER 20

Building Maturity

Using effective discipleship in relationships to enhance the ministry locally and corporately is essential for building maturity individually and collectively.

Though there are many ways to learn and grow, doing so efficiently adds value and expediency to the ministry as a whole. Teaching is most efficient when it is done individually and in small groups. Many churches have little they can reference in the way of intimate relationship-building programs or paradigms. As I have mentioned in the sections on evangelism and leadership prospecting, discipline and focus need to be fundamental components in building intimate discipling relationships as well. This too, is an area that is far too often left to "chance and luck." To train people to be good mentors, to speak truthfully, to handle conflict and so forth must be taught proactively, carefully, maturely, and deliberately. Relationship-building will ultimately bear upon the long-term viability of a ministry or a church.

Bible Study is the building block that all believers should be building on.

One should be vigilant that a lack of discipline in the daily practice of developing a relationship with God does not infiltrate his or her Bible study. Bible study is and should be the absolute foundation of all Christians do to develop themselves and preserve their personal faith and relationship with God. Bible study is the primary source of any substantial knowledge of the true character and persona of God. In the following segment of this chapter, I have included some interesting statistics on "bible study" in general to help illustrate some of the points I am trying to convey.

Bible Ownership

Most Americans own a Bible. In fact, 92 percent of households in America own at least one copy. Of those households that own a Bible, the average number of Bibles is three. This includes not only the homes of practicing Christians but hundreds of thousands of atheists as well.[1]

Bible Reading

Although most Americans own a Bible, they do not all use it the same way. A poll taken by the Gallup Organization in October, 2000 found that 59percent of Americans reported that they read the Bible at least occasionally. This number represents a 73 percent decrease from the 1980s. The same poll found that 37 percent of Americans read the Bible at least once a week. This number represents a 40 percent decrease from 1990.[2] According to the Barna Research Group, those who read the Bible regularly spend about 52 minutes a week studying the scriptures.[3] Barna, "The Bible," data is from 1997.

Which gender is more faithful at reading the Bible at least weekly? The prize goes to the women. While 42 percent of women have read the Bible in the past week, only 32 percent of men have done the same.[4] In addition, as of 1997, those who read the Bible preferred the King James Version to the New International Version by a five-to-one margin.[5]

Bible Study

When it comes to going beyond merely reading the Bible to actually studying it, the numbers decline sharply. Only one in seven Americans report an involvement that goes beyond just reading the Bible. Fourteen percent of

Americans currently belong to a Bible study group.[6] This number represents a 33 percent decrease from 1990, when 21 percent of respondents said they were involved in a Bible study group. [7]

Bible Knowledge

How about knowledge of the Bible? According to Gallup, "Despite the impressive statistics concerning Bible reading and study, it is apparent that ignorance about its contents is widespread."[8]

More evidences for this conclusion include:

- Only half of adults interviewed nationwide could name any of the four Gospels of the New Testament.
- Only 37 percent of those interviewed could name all four Gospels.
- Only 42 percent of adults were able to name as many as five of the Ten Commandments correctly.
- 7 in 10 respondents (70 percent) were able to name the town where Jesus was born, and only 42 percent could identify him as the person who delivered the Sermon on the Mount.[9]

Researcher George Barna has also documented the lack of Bible knowledge in the United States:

- 38 percent of Americans believe the entire Bible was written several decades after Jesus's death and resurrection (While this is true of the New Testament, the entire Old Testament was written hundreds of years before the birth of Jesus Christ).

- 12 percent of adults believe that Noah's wife was Joan of Arc.
- 49 percent believe the Bible teaches that money is the root of all evil, when in fact it teaches that the love of money is the root of all types of evil.
- 75 percent believe the Bible teaches that God helps those who help themselves. [10]

George Lindbeck, the famous Yale theologian, has commented on the decreasing knowledge of scripture from a professor's perspective: "When I first arrived at Yale, even those who came from nonreligious backgrounds knew the Bible better than most of those now who come from churchgoing families." [11]

Recent research highlights the decreasing influence of the Bible in the United States and the declining importance of serious Bible study by Christians. As our society becomes increasingly pluralistic and subjective in its worldview, the more important it will be for Christians to know and study their Bible. Only by doing so can we intelligently present a biblical worldview to those who know so little of the soul-saving Word.

Sadly, many who claim to be Christians are Biblically ignorant and lack even a rudimentary knowledge of the Bible. Of even greater concern is the prevalence of Biblical illiteracy amongst teens. In order for a ministry to survive, it must emphasize the importance of regular, disciplined Bible study.

Imitation is a very effective and underrated way to learn.

Jesus' greatest teaching tool was his life. The most effective vehicle by which He was able to display His life was through relationships.

Living a lifestyle that reflects our beliefs distinguishes true Christians from the hypocritical Pharisees of whom the Bible speaks. The Pharisees were a group of highly educated and respected religious authorities in Jesus' day who taught very harsh adherence to enhanced and embellished codes of religious conduct loosely based on the Old Testament bible. The Pharisees were feared by many until Jesus came and challenged them openly about their rampant hypocrisy and strict religious by-laws.

When a ministry leader lives a life that reflects his faith, his integrity will not only validate his authority; it will also inspire others to follow his example. People will consciously and unconsciously imitate what they see. If a leader sets a bad example, his flock will be more apt to challenge his agenda or disregard his leadership. On the other hand, because popular culture encourages the public not to challenge authority, a ministry leader's flock might emulate his arrogant, self-preserving machinations as well without challenge or accountability. Such a scenario leads to the inevitable destruction of a ministry. In order to avoid it, a leader would do well to bear in mind the axiom that a man will reap what he sows. If he proffers a virtuous example, he will expedite his followers' own progress toward leadership and spiritual maturation. One of the most effective lesson plans I have used is having Christians analyze certain characters in the bible with an aim toward finding that character they themselves can imitate. This approach is handy in that is both uses the Bible as a teaching tool and helps to bring Biblical characters to life for one's students. In getting to know the bible more, you will find most all of the characters in it very relatable.

Gentle accountability and follow-up will insure a greater degree of success in your discipleship and leadership.

An effective leader never guesses whether people have carried out one of his directives or assumes that people are fully committed to growing with God. Deuteronomy chapter eight teaches that Christians will always benefit from gentle, caring reminders about important quotidian matters. Like non-believers, many Christians struggle with discipline; therefore, a wise leader would do well not only to be alert to signs that members are faltering in their follow-through, but also to act decisively when the need arises. Many ministry leaders make the mistake of thinking lessons taught once through a sermon or group study will sustain his members' discipline regarding studying the scriptures and living a virtuous lifestyle. In my view, the assumption is false. If the goal is to grow the ministry, follow-up is essential. It gets things done and reinforces information transferred in the corporate setting. People who make success a priority—whether their efforts are in business, marriage, other interpersonal relationships, or education—understand the importance of follow-up, which is as essential for ministry as it is for secular endeavors. In my opinion, the prevailing culture of Christian ministry-building has trivialized the discipline of follow-up as an insignificant and unspiritual undertaking.

Push yourself by aiming for a new personal best in setting new and more challenging goals.

Goals, dreams and visions are, by definition, meant to be attained. However, integral to the process of attainment is re-evaluation. A wise leader never hesitates to set new goals when he achieves initial goals and fulfills his original vision. Continuing to challenge oneself can not only keep at bay the mediocrity and complacency that can be so detrimental to a Christian's growth but also ward off spirit of arrogance which can accompany success—the attitude that one "has arrived" and need not go any further to be closer to God and his people.

Build a spirit of healthy and fun competition to stimulate greater growth collectively and individually.

Have fun with your peers and comrades while building ministry. Most everyone loves sports and other competitive games like cards, chess, dominoes, and so forth. No one ever said that ministry-building had to be onerous , boring and non-interactive. On the contrary, creating a light atmosphere of competition brings members closer while they strive to excel by pushing each other to greater degrees of excellence. Specific techniques for making ministry fun are limited only by one's imaginative abilities and experiences. To get the ball rolling, a ministry leader might observe what others are doing in their ministries, especially if their approach is working well, and adapt some of the techniques to his own unique ministry situation.

Motivating people by using their inherent human nature is not only productive and efficient, but character-building as well. People want to excel and see success in measurable outcomes. Tapping into people's desire to build something noteworthy—whether in their ministry, profession, or personal life—is an effective way to help Christians stay motivated in their journey toward excellence, discipline, and maturity. In the words of the apostle Paul in 2 Timothy 4:7-I have fought the good fight, I have finished the race and kept the faith. Another Pauline passage of inspiration is 1 Corinthians 9:26 where he speaks of not fighting for your faith in vain. Both of these passages show us Paul's emphasis on fighting for our faith in God effectively and with purpose. A wise leader teaches people to learn from others who are excelling, build upon small successes, and apply tried-and-true strategies to unfamiliar situations. Success breeds success. With joy and optimism, explore the full range of cooperative learning strategies in order to energize oneself and one's ministry.

*Statistical excerpts (with bibliography) courtesy of:
Americans and the Bible:
Bible Ownership, Reading, Study and Knowledge in the United States
by Michael J. Vlach
Theologicalstudies.org

1 George Gallup, Jr., The Role of the Bible in American Society (Princeton: The Princeton ReligionResearch Center, 1990)

2 Barna Research Online, "The Bible," www.barna.org. This information is based on 1993 figures.

3 Alec Gallup and Wendy W. Simmons, "Six in Ten Americans Read Bible at Least Occasionally," TheGallup Organization, www.gallup.com, October 20, 2000.

4 Barna, "The Bible," data is from 1997.

5 Ibid., data is from 2001.

6 Gallup, "Six in Ten Americans Read Bible at

7 Gallup, The Role of the Bible in American Society, 17.

8 Ibid.

9 Ibid.

10 Barna, "The Bible," The information is from the years 1994, 1997, 1994, and 2000 respectively.

11 George A. Lindbeck, "The Church's Mission to a Postmodern Culture," Postmodern Theology: ChristianFaith in a Pluralist World (San Francisco: Harper & Row Publishers, 1989) 45.

CHAPTER 21

Building Maturity in Pragmatic Terms

Give homework assignments and make learning fun, creative and interactive.

Give the Christians in your ministry some materials and suggestions for enhancing their "walk with God" on their own. Many Christians struggle with developing a personal curriculum, so be willing to make suggestions with assignments they can do at home. Through discipleship and relationship-building, delegate responsibility to others. For example, keeping in mind that the ultimate goals is not so much a matter of telling members what to study as HOW to study (remember: we are more interested in process over results) and maximize study time. One might delegate to mature ministry leaders the responsibility of teaching others how to become independent learners. By emphasizing process over product, a ministry leader is able not only to tap into under-utilized talent, but also to convert his members to his specific pedagogical philosophy.

Scripture memorization is as effective and essential for the mind as it is the heart.

Satan's greatest tool against Christians is his own knowledge of God's word coupled with most believers' overall lack of biblical knowledge. It is appalling that most who consider themselves Christians know so little about the Bible—the only source of knowledge about God's true character and His promises. A ministry leader should consistently reinforce the importance of personal Bible study so that his ministry can grow spiritually individually and collectively. Many leaders do not enforce this practice with their ministry members because they themselves lack the discipline to practice , memorize and apply scripture regularly themselves. Remember, Satan's greatest ploy is to take scripture and twist it. He knows the Word of thoroughly and completely. Christians who do not know their Bible fall prey to Satan's deception more easily than those who do not. In Matthew 4:1-11 of the biblical gospels, we see the timeless story of Jesus walking in the desert for 40 days and nights in prologue to actively starting His ministry. The resounding theme I want to emphasize from this story and adventure of Jesus is His personal confrontations with Satan. In every instance Satan uses scriptures twisted contextually in attempts to deceive Jesus. Jesus counters every scriptural jab thrown by Satan by using scripture as well. Two of the greatest powers in existence here in this passage wage war with scripture at the root of it all. A true believer of God stands very little if any chance of spiritual survival without any working and intimate knowledge of the Word of God to say the least.

The concept of "Studying" scripture.

Bible study requires patience and persistence no less than any other life goal worth attaining. Many have a desire but lack the tools or knowledge of how to study anything. As leaders, we must teach people to develop study habits that take into consideration that fact that life with God can be a "marathon". People will "drop out of the race" if not encouraged to grow in this particular discipline. A scripture that emphasizes the importance and value to the apostle Paul about diligent study of God's Word can be found in Acts 17:10-12 where Paul commends the Bereans for their deep, constant and consistent study of the scriptures. Paul even goes on to deem this discipline of deep diligent study as "noble charactered".

Study different leaders in the bible. Chances are you will find them to be just like you and me in so many ways! Learn from them and about them.

The Bible presents many leaders whose character can be an example and many others whose character can be a warning. Teach people to discern the difference and apply the lessons to their own lives. In Ecclesiastes 1:9 of the Old Testament, we find Solomon's very tried and true words of great wisdom: "what has been will be again, what has been done will be done again. There is nothing new under the sun." Except for some "cosmetics" regarding the ancient dates and times many of these biblical character's lived, very little has changed in the specifics of human nature, interaction and social discourse in comparison to the modern day. Though many of these biblical stories and their participants had different and somewhat unique situations, you will find a great deal of relevance and connection with the thoughts, feelings and actions of many of these personalities.

It is wise to develop some basic debate skills and a working knowledge of simple apologetics as a leader. Learn to use the Word of God as a true weapon!

Because the subject of God is so very controversial and polarizing, ministry leaders should acquaint themselves with basic debate techniques so that they will be prepared to handle contention and disagreement. I know from my personal experience with evangelism that any Christian who has never had an argument or a contentious moment in conversation about God, has yet to share his faith about the God I have read about in the bible. In this aspect of leader preparation as in others, leave nothing to chance. Train and prepare for moments of debate regarding your faith and belief in God.

This whole concept of teaching basic debate based on a growing and working knowledge of God's Word can be fun and exhilarating as well as educational depending on how you format your training. This can be a wonderful time to group together a class of young and potential leaders, create an atmosphere of learning, competition and spiritual purpose while also forging relationships that will affect them for many years in a positive and meaningful way. I have my personal "tried and true" methods that I use. I will leave you with this "lump of clay" to shape and mold yourself.

As a leader, you will find some basic knowledge in pubic and persuasive speaking of great value.

God's kingdom always has a need for good public speakers. However, many people are intimidated by public speaking and have very little knowledge of effective techniques. Even so, ministry leaders responsible for training must teach this skill in keeping with the specific responsibilities of the novices under their supervision.

As a leader teaches effective communication skills vis-à-vis public speaking, he must be careful to include instructing in the art of listening, which is an essential part of being a good conversationalist. So many leaders like to go straight into "preach and fix" mode. Though some might be receptive to this approach, many will get turned off. When people seek advice for a personal problem, they want a confidante, someone who will be understanding and discreet. Therefore, it is of the utmost importance that a ministry leader project an aura of patience, integrity, and discretion so that his ability to listen will not only give him an inroad to a potential convert's heart, but also help the supplicant identify his own problems and find his own solutions.

Learning to be a great listener and conversationalist in general will be of great use during times when a ministry leader will have to referee his ministry's internal conflicts. Asking questions, being patient, and admitting that he does not have all the answers will keep a ministry leader in good stead whether he is directly involved in a conflict or only mediating a conflict among others. Also, it is also a good idea to ask for time to think about all sides of an issue and to bear in mind that few people are gifted with the special communication skills that effective conflict mediation requires. Most people have to learn them. In a more public setting, such as a small group setting, having a good sense of listening to the comments and questions being made can help an experienced leader tailor his/ her discussion in a direction that would be most pertinent at the moment as well as set up very effective fellowship time after the formal group. Whether in a personal, small group or mediation scenario, listening with the intent to understand will reap great fruit and results.

Learning to think under pressure is of great value since that will become a predominant part of a leader's reality.

Senior leadership is responsible for training subordinate leaders to deal with as many scenarios as possible insuring a greater degree of success and competency in contrast to just throwing someone into the role of leadership with a "good luck and God will take care of the rest" methodology which unfortunately seems to actually be the norm. Role-playing, thinking through hypothetical scenarios in small groups, and allowing trainees to experiment with leadership within the group as an assistant are effective ways of preparing them to handle potential leadership responsibilities within a safe and supportive context regarding the various scenarios that will inevitably arise. Letting people experience leadership within a peer group tests and refines their ability to handle their anticipated responsibilities in a very "real-time"/ "real- life" setting. It should never be assumed that people are able to think under pressure and lead spiritually without any training or prior exposure to common scenarios.

Teach people the process of "learning".

Most of us have been trained to please a teacher by coming up with the "right answers." However, recent scholarship in educational psychology has shown that teacher- and lecture-centered pedagogy is less effective than student- and inquiry-based pedagogy in achieving learning outcomes. In fact, teacher- and lecture- centered pedagogy can be counter-productive and lead to arrogance and legalism. Proverbs chapter 1 teaches that the process of seeking and searching is what leads to wisdom. To punctuate my point in this segment, Luke 11:1-4 shows a great example of the apostles displaying a great "learners heart" when they say to Jesus-please teach us to pray just a John taught his disciples. The amazing irony to this story is that a group of religious Jewish men who have been praying since childhood were asking this young single Jesus how to pray.

A leader can and should always depend on the Bible as his exclusive reference and foundation of all things spiritual in his life and ministry.

*****

The following introduction is made up of a few "bullet points" to set the tone for this next section discussing the importance of having the bible as the proprietary sole standard and foundation of any ministry endeavor.

- When things get confusing and difficult, the Bible gives clarity through spiritual simplicity.

  Philippians 4:6-9 states: "Do not be anxious about anything, but in everything, by prayer and petition, with thanksgiving, present your requests to God. 7 And the peace of God, which transcends all understanding, will guard your hearts and your minds in Christ Jesus. 8 Finally, brothers, whatever is true, whatever is noble, whatever is right, whatever is pure, whatever is lovely, whatever is admirable -- if anything is excellent or praiseworthy -- think about such things. 9 Whatever you have learned or received or heard from me, or seen in me -- put it into practice. And the God of peace will be with you." (This scripture is especially important because it emphasizes my point of "simplicity" when things seem to be getting very complex and confusing.)

- When controversies and arguments arise, the Bible can mediate them.

  Titus 3:9-11 states: but avoid foolish controversies and genealogies and arguments and quarrels about the law because these are unprofitable and useless.

- When animosity and division threaten, the Bible can conquer it.

  Titus 3:10-11 states: warn a divisive person once and then warn them a second time. After that, have nothing to do with them. You may be sure that such people are warped and sinful; they are self-condemned.

- When myths and hersy emerge, the Bible dispels them.

  1 Timothy 4:7 states: have nothing to do with Godless myths and old wives tales; rather, train yourself to be Godly. (complete scripture in 1 Timothy 4:2-12 gives very supportive and substantive explanation to the entire text regarding this particular point.

- In sum, the Bible must be the foundation of a ministry and the absolute standard for each and every facet of its being.

  2 Timothy 3:16-17 states: All scripture is God-breathed and is useful for teaching, rebuking, correcting and training in righteousness so that the man of God may be thoroughly equipped for every good work.

All the above points, questions and dilemmas can be dealt with if a ministry leader puts time and effort into establishing the Bible as the absolute standard and authority from the very beginning.

A ministry leader's expectations regarding the role of the Bible within the ministry should be simple , direct and completely understood: Those who do not or cannot accept the Word of God as the absolute standard should not be a part of any Christian leadership or membership (this does not include people were are sharing our faith with or unbelieving visitors.). By visiting different churches, I have found that many are winning converts even though they do not take this tenet seriously. But make no mistake: A ministry not built upon the Bible as its sole foundation—especially if the ministry leader does not hold himself and others to that principle—will surely crumble. People in leadership, or even ministry members in non-leadership positions, who do not hold to the Bible as an absolute standard, may dilute the Bible's simple message with a variety of "clinical" methodologies, myths, half-truths, second-hand anecdotes and personal opinions. In such a climate, what begins as a slow process of erosion can quickly accelerate so as to put the entire ministry on the fast track to destruction.

CHAPTER 22

Lean and Mean!

Size and scope of a small group bible talk or ministry can determine the overall potential for growth, mobility and general flexibility. The following section deals with efficiency in small group structure, physical appearance and a more effective functionality dynamic.

No small group or small ministry "blobs" will have any long term effective viability.

People usually do not work hard if they know they can hide and let someone else do the work. This dynamic often emerges in congregations where the ministry leader prefers to preside over the congregants' spiritual development exclusively from the pulpit, thus leading the whole congregation as one large "small group" or as I like to refer to it: a "bible blob". This approach is arrogant, immature, and ineffective. This approach is preferred by many ministers because it saves them the work of having to train new leaders. It also preserves their overall authority by not having to delegate leadership and other responsibilities to others. These are harsh words, but I choose them deliberately in order to point out that the most effective and spiritual strategy for any ministry is to delegate responsibility by tapping into its reserve of latent talent rather than allow one individual to arrogate all power to himself, as in a monarchy, or to a small, select group, as in an oligarchy. This kind of traditional leadership dynamic usually results in overall limited growth, "bottlenecking" and dogma. We must question our hearts as leaders when we are not willing to share our authority and leadership with others to shepherd God's people into a closer relationship with Him and other Christians. When leaders take it upon themselves to be the "grand task master" or sole aggregate or "medium" to whom God has given an exclusive mandate to lead His people, cultic tendencies can develop.

Everyone should be gently held accountable for working in their respective small groups.

It takes work to build anything including a kingdom. In this case specifically, it takes work to build God's Kingdom. Nowhere in the bible dies God's Kingdom or His modern church use any allusion or imagery to describe serving God by following Jesus as a vacation or tropical getaway. Gently keeping people accountable for the work that has to be done to build God's church by keeping our obligation to contribute, motivated by grace and gratitude, will insure a healthy culture and attitude amongst the members of your respective ministry.

Small groups, amongst the many effective things they can accomplish, can also create the conditions for leaders to be raised up and trained more quickly for the life of the ministry to be monitored with greater simplicity. In other words, the small-group paradigm allows a leader to shepherd his flock more effectively and efficiently. In the book of Exodus chapter 18 beginning in verse 13, we see that Moses, who was personally chosen by God to lead, had to be taught and admonished to delegate, train and trust other reliable men to help him lead the nation of Israel in their newly liberated society.

It is peculiar to me that so many ministry leaders, who have this very well-known story and lesson available to them, would continue to fall into the age-old tradition of practicing hierarchical and empirical leadership with the overwhelming biblical evidences of how unspiritual and ineffective this is. Our egos can blind us to so many personal and ministry-collective needs!

Keep small groups SMALL for greater effectiveness.

Another advantage of the small-group paradigm is that it renders more efficient the ongoing tasks of observation, evaluation, and if necessary, revision—especially when those tasks are undertaken with an aim toward accomplishing specific goals. Increasing a congregation's membership and attendance numbers, helping current members grow spiritually, promoting a better flow of communication and sustaining a ministry's long-term viability can be just some of many present and potential goals a leader will accomplish more effectively and efficiently on a small group level.

Small groups: "epicenter of communication"

A church's spiritual and community-outreach work should be delegated to small groups exclusively with an aim toward maximized efficiency and effectiveness. A reason for this is that small groups are easier to organize, mobilize and communicate with. Evangelizing, team-building, and carrying out specific Bible-based activities and objectives, just to name a few ministry building activities, are best handled at the small-group level. In addition, the small group enables congregants to process, through focused discussion and targeted activities, spiritual concepts and directives from "higher up" in the chain of communication. In sum, small groups function as an "Epicenter of communication."

Another effective functionality of small groups is that it acts as an "Incubator" for leaders.

A church should select and train its core leadership and cultivate subordinate leaders in the safety and homogeneity of a small group environment. Much like an incubator, a small group can function as a controlled and "safe" dynamic by which assistant and potential leaders can be observed, trained and even prospected for future responsibilities regarding work in God's church in a much more "real time" and real life environment. In a small group, both observation, delegation and evaluation are drastically simplified regarding training and prospecting.

A small group can provide a trainer and oversight teacher/ leader the opportunity, otherwise to difficult and complicated in a large corporate structure, to delegate responsibilities to potential and developing leaders for purposes of training in reliability, efficiency and maturity. A small group environment can also provide great opportunities to "prospect" potential leaders and workers by observing firsthand in a smaller dynamic those who display an assertive and aggressive attitude towards service. Those who show a penchant for being self-motivated with a strong work ethic are obvious candidates for future responsibilities in service for God.

Corporate and large group growth will be handles most effectively through small group division and organization.

A church should train its leaders with an aim toward preparing them to handle the fruits of numerical growth. The more people that have a part and responsibility (ownership) in the growing ministry, and the more they feel useful and a part of the forward progress of the ministry, the greater the ministry's synergistic energy will be. The feeling of excitement and productivity that comes with collective ownership will help to facilitate a perpetual culture of forward momentum. It is most effective to delegate and facilitate the work and responsibilities of leaders as well as the ministry in general on a smaller, more localized level such as a small group. This dynamic will simplify and streamline the process of integrating new members into the fold with greater effect rather than handling everything on the large group, corporate levels as most ministers like to do continuing the traditional and ineffective practice of leading via an empirical oligarchy under a hierarchical model.

Expansion and conquest through division: keep dividing things down staying true to the vision of a more simple, effective and streamline ministry dynamic as you encompass greater growth.

A church should anticipate expansion and plan to divide groups as they grow larger. It should keep its subordinate ministries “lean and mean” in order to keep the emphasis on intimate relationships as the primary conduit for advancing God’s message. The multiplication of groups highlights a ministry’s expansion, which keeps its members motivated and prevents the overall spirit of the ministry from stagnating.

A church leader(s) would be wise to not let a ministry that was conceived as small group grow past a certain number. One good reason to keep a ministry numerically small is that when groups get too large, those on the margins feel the central power weakly. As people move out of the central power’s orbit of an “overgrown” ministry group, individual personalities, nepotism, and sycophantism may become the ties that eventually bind. Consequently, a cliquish, ego-driven climate may emerge. Such a climate can hamper the ability of new members who are saved to reach out and prevent new members who are not saved from being reached. As I mentioned previously, larger groups enable people who have lost their motivation to “hide” in the chaos of a group too large to organize efficiently. Though the reasons for a decline in motivation may vary—insecurity, pride, laziness, and so on—it is easier to help people overcome these character defects when their supporting community remains small and manageable enough for them to have significant and meaningful interaction. Allowing members to lose focus and consequently fall "through the cracks" in a large fellowship, usually disorganized , stagnant and impersonal as I have experienced all too many times, will prove discouraging and counterproductive in the long term. The best course for a leader who knows the importance of not leaving anything to chance is to view fellowship as yet another opportunity to support the corporate body's mission by training congregants in the ways of effective, productive and fruitful fellowship in God's kingdom. A large fellowship left to chance with no training, direction or discipline amounts to nothing more than a large "cocktail social". In contrast, smaller groups (ideally five to ten people) enable both abstract and concrete goals to materialize within a controlled—and therefore more efficient—environment.

If we take a moment to analyze most of the four Gospels in the New Testament of the Bible, you will find that Jesus himself gave us the original model of small group ministry, as His way of initiating, organizing and galvanizing his own ministry commensurate, by his choosing and travelling with His apostles and several women almost exclusively. He went even further by becoming close to just a few within the group of 12. I will expound upon this thought with further scriptural reference in my conclusion.

Groups can move around to different locations and activity centers with greater ease if kept to a manageable number allowing for greater mobility.

Small group allow for the greatest amount of manageable flexibility.

Activities and themes for a small-group ministry are bound only by the leader's imagination and that of the group. Activities should be fun and get as many people as possible involved. Having this kind of creative synergy can only happen when leadership has the time and space needed through a very manageable and streamline ministry to be flexible with all of the different ideas and inputs offered by such an active ministry. One litmus test to assess a ministry's flexibility is how disagreements and problems are handled when they arise. A corporate ministry divided into manageable parts will enable conflicts to be resolved more efficiently and expeditiously than they can be at the corporate level, where problems can fester and, though they may take more time to develop, can become quite destructive once they have touched enough people and gathered enough momentum. Small- group and local ministries act as a type of "firewall" to stop small "problems" before they snowball and steamroll the entire corporate body.

Small groups also allow for better and more effective communication. When leadership on all levels of a ministry are linked via an agreed-upon chain of communication. Information originating from the corporate tier can be transmitted and processed at each subdivision in whatever way is most appropriate for individual groups. In other words, small groups allow information to be personalized to a degree that is not possible when a member of corporate leadership makes an announcement in an open forum or "sends out a flyer". Small groups also create accountability because they make follow-up organized and effective.

Intimacy, fellowship and multifaceted relationship dynamics are easier to initiate and maintain on the small group levels.

In order to maximize the effectiveness and efficiency of growth, leaders of subdivisions may link some aspects of their programs to other subdivisions. The combined effort allows them to make a greater impact on the corporate level. Combining efforts on the sub-local levels improves their own health as well as that of the overall body. Building relationships through mentor- and discipleship is best accomplished in either small groups of five to ten people or individual partnerships. Facilitating the conditions and vision for intimacy in mentor-mentee relationships insures that the corporate body will receive, on the cellular level, the spiritual nourishment it needs to grow. Churches do not usually erode or fall apart because of problems in the corporate dynamic. More often, they begin to disintegrate on the cellular level where individuals are not tied into the body in a healthy way. The value of small groups and their overall purpose and functionality in furthering the corporate vision and commensurate cannot be overstated as we have mentioned in just a few instances here in conclusion of this section.

Conversions: the role of the small group ministry in nurturing those who have made the decision to give their lives and hearts to God.

How a person comes to God can vary as much as each individual can. Although conversions (biblically speaking-an adult of consenting age who makes a conscious, rational and responsible decision to give their life to God) often happen in the large-group setting, small groups should be responsible for creating the conditions for a recent convert to sustain his commitment to the faith over time to utilize the greatest amount of ministry efficiency. At the small-group level, those who are new in the faith can be paired with those who are more mature in their faith for Bible study and other activities designed to build and sustain a new convert's relationship with both God and his fellow parishioners, who can, along with the small-group leader, transmit corporate-level communiqués in a way that is most appropriate for new converts at their particular stage of development. The entire process, from first to last, is designed to give new converts access to the full range of resources available on all ministry levels and thereby maximize his long-term success.

Fostering Discipling Relationships: taking fellowship to greater levels of intimacy and maturity.

Teaching, encouraging, and creating a gentle atmosphere of accountability are accomplished most effectively on the local level, as in a small-group ministry, than they are on the macro level of church organization. Small-group settings allow a ministry to formulate goals, design a strategy for achieving them, teach, and share experiences in a way that creates the synergy needed to maintain the ministry's viability and maximize its impact on the larger community where it exists. This energy also transfers directly to the corporate body and perpetuates energy on all levels of ministry.

Initiating relationships with the desire for them to evolve into close friendships and building them on a biblical foundation are ideal goals for a person to have when he enters into a mentor-mentee relationship. Bonds of discipleship should nurture both parties spiritually, perpetuate the maturation of their faith, and generally be a "safe place", spiritually speaking, for the parties to grow in their relationship to God and others. It is again notable, Jesus' conduct in the Gospels setting the standard for discipleship, intimacy in relationships and small group dynamics. He disseminates his ideas primarily by transmitting his spiritual message to His close three (Peter, James and John), the 12 apostles, the seventy-two, and so forth. One could argue that His first objective after he had spent forty days in the desert was NOT just to convert the "world" to his ideas primarily, but to cultivate and develop a small group (ministry) that would serve as his spiritual aggregator of sorts: He found his "intimate three" in James, John and Peter; the Twelve; the Seventy-Two, and so on (John 4:1-2) as an example . Similarly, churches will maximize their ability to cultivate closeness and strengthen the bonds of spiritual intimacy among its members by concentrating on the micro rather than the macro level of organization. Consequently, it is on the corporate level that one will see the return on his investment in small-group development. Specifically, corporate-level meetings will be characterized by vibrancy, spontaneity and zeal. The fellowship following a corporate meeting will be the result of the care and sensitivity cultivated through local level relationship-building activities. The desired results on the corporate level will materialize only to the extent that a church emphasizes the importance of relationship-building strategies on the local levels, provides its sub-divisions with the tools necessary to accomplish stated objectives, and devises a system of accountability and an instrument for measuring progress on every level of the church.

CHAPTER 23

What role can the small group ministry effectively play?

When someone wants to make the decision to give his or her life to God, a small group ministry can play a very important role.

Based on years of experience and observation, I believe that what churches do with the public alter call is not very effective, or even biblical, as far as drawing people to God for reconciliation. A number of experts and evangelical leadership groups have commented on this very subject. For example, Kirk Cameron and Ray Comfort cite a number of sources supporting the thesis above:

> Charles E. Hackett, National Director for the Assemblies of God, Division of Home Missions says, "A soul at the altar does not generate much excitement in some circles because we realize approximately ninety-five out of every hundred will not become integrated into the church. In fact, most of them will not return for a second visit."
>
> In his book Today's Evangelism, Ernest C. Reisinger says of one outreach event, "It lasted eight days, and there were sixty-eight supposed conversions." A month later, not one of the "converts" could be found.
>
> In 1991, organizers of a Salt Lake City concert encouraged follow-up. They said, "Less then 5 percent of

those who respond to an altar call during a public crusade . . . are living a Christian life one year later." In other words, more than 95 percent proved to be false converts.

A pastor in Boulder, Colorado, sent a team to Russia in 1991 and obtained 2,500 decisions. The next year, the team found only thirty continuing in their faith. That's a retention rate of 1.2 percent.

In November 1970, a number of churches combined for a convention in Fort Worth, Texas, and secured 30,000 decisions. Six months later, the follow-up committee could find only thirty continuing in their faith.

A mass crusade reported 18,000 decisions—yet according to Church Growth magazine, 94 percent failed to become incorporated into a local church.

In Sacramento, California, a combined crusade yielded more than 2,000 commitments. One church followed up on fifty-two of those decisions and couldn't find one true convert.

A leading U.S. denomination reported that during 1995 it secured 384,057 decisions but retained only 22,983 in fellowship. The church could not account for 361,074 supposed conversions. That's a 94 percent fall-away rate.

In the March/April 1993 issue of American Horizon, the national director of home missions of a major U.S. denomination disclosed that in 1991, 11,500 churches had obtained 294,784 decisions for Christ. Unfortunately, they could find only 14,337 in fellowship. That means that

> despite the usual intense follow-up, they could not account for approximately 280,000 of their "converts."

* These reproduced statistical excerpts are courtesy of:

The Modern Invitation System Examined: The reality of false conversions by: Massimo Lorenzini- Frontline Ministries

Frontlinemin.org

* Original statistical study by:

Kirk Cameron and Ray Comfort, The Way of the Master (Wheaton, Ill.: Tyndale House Publishers, 2004), pp. 61-63.

If reconciliation with God is a matter of intimacy, meditation, cost counting, and so forth, people need a more intimate setting wherein these goals can be accomplished and the commitment sustained over time. With exception to Pentecostal environments, where the hype and emotions of the moment may overwhelm the bottom line—sincere and long-term commitment to the faith—the most effective conversions I have seen are those that have been done in a small "community" setting such as a family or intimate small group where the convert was introduced to God through many aspects of this concentrated fellowship, brought to the waters of baptism and then ,most importantly, nourished and strengthened to spiritual good health and maturity in the safety and confines of this same small group setting.

Again, I must reiterate that everything I suggest finds its way back to the importance of delegating leadership and accomplishing the ministry's most critical goals at the small-group level. A minister who insists upon controlling the church exclusively or mostly from the pulpit actually cripples the church's collective ability to accomplish its overarching mission by facilitating the spiritual maturation of each individual and igniting their passion for the church's daily work. I am ,of course, referring to the ineffective "alter call" tradition most churches have adopted to help people make a decision to follow God. Instead of delegating the work of helping people make such a profound decision and getting many involved, many ministers, as they lead in so many areas of their own respective ministries', have used this age old tradition of alter calls because it safely protects and insulates their leadership and authority in a vacuum thus continuing and propagating the endless and destructive cycle of "empirical" leadership. An unhealthy obsession with control may be a warning sign of "cultic" tendencies in talented, charismatic ministers who experience a great deal of success by doing everything themselves. When you take into consideration the emotionally charged "show" most alter calls have become, the almost electrifying dogma of a charismatic minister and the spiritual and emotional vulnerability of one who wants desperately to find a closer relationship with God and you now have a recipe for disaster, spiritually speaking.

As an example, to proactively delegate the work and to cultivate a sense of collective ownership amongst your collective ministry (and not just one or a few leaders), in regards to "soul-winning", an individual church member might be given the charge to issue a blanket invitation immediately following a Sunday service for potential converts to attend a small group bible study to examine the story of the Cross (as just an example) in the Gospels of the Bible one-on-one with trusted church members. Whatever specific course one pursues, the important thing to keep in mind is that small groups are the most effective place to counsel people who want to study and count cost regarding discipleship, and that small groups contain all the components needed to nurture and retain new converts: intimacy; solid, maintainable relationships; a post-baptismal support system, and so forth. Through the small group, in their quest to help "save the lost", you will not only be helping the lost find God, but you will also be helping the believers in that particular ministry find great joy and ownership by doing the work God called ALL believers to do.

Though the pulpit or senior minister can and should be present when a small group is hosting people who are close to conversion, the small-group or local level leader should be empowered to preside over the conversions in their own respective ministries.. Leaving proselytization in the hands of small-group leadership is the surest way for a church to ensure that membership will grow in terms of multiplication rather than addition and subtraction, the growth trend that most often results from monarchical and oligarchical modes of leadership so widely accepted as the norm in today's church.

I also believe that steering people (especially youth) toward an interactive website with instant messaging and blogging capabilities will net more people who might be ready to make a decision but lack the confidence to approach someone directly. To further punctuate my point of creatively trying to get as many people involved in the work of "soul winning", setting up programs such as a website, blog, group activities, etc is a, effective way of building synergy and ownership among those in your ministries. A leader will have to "crucify" his/ her own ego tied to "leadership" in order to let others spearhead many of these creative reach out strategies and activities.

To conclude, a church should give people multiple approaches (including a public invitation) for coming to God. As a church grows and its membership multiplies, it should constantly reassess the efficacy of all of its programs and protocols in terms of their success in accomplishing key objectives. To continue with the analogy between Jesus as a fisher of men and the Church as a savior of souls, it difficult to catch fish with a net full of holes.

CHAPTER 24

Follow up moves the world!

In this chapter I will suggest some effective "follow-up" techniques. The concept of "follow-up" is very effective and unique. I believe that true follow up as a conviction and a discipline separates effective evangelism and general communication from surface conversation that fails to materialize ultimately becoming fruitless banter and rhetoric. I have rarely seen, in all of my years of visiting many different ministries, a church or specific ministry use the practice and discipline of follow-up as a key component of fellowship or ministry outreach, general and inter-ministry communication. This "golden thread" weaves through all programs to hold them together in order to make them practical and effective by way of synergistic, proactive and continual communications.

Years ago, I heard a saying that applies very well to ministry communications (internal as well as external): "Dreamers and visionaries inspire only for a moment, while follow-up moves the world." Too few leaders (I am surprised and sad to say) I have found are trained or familiar in the basic, disciplined practice of follow-up. Here are several examples of what I am trying to say about the subject of communication follow-up. If you have a romantic interest in someone, you will not go far with it if you leave all potential of a special relationship to a single meeting at a social gathering and never call him or her! If you want to make a significant purchase such as a house, car, college, travel package, or something of the like, you will need to follow up multiple times in order to close the deal by continuing to secure a better understanding and pricing agreement for the potential purchase. Similarly, Christians' ongoing mandate to save the lost and keep the saved saved requires follow-up as well. However, in my own personal observation and experience, many churches and small-group ministries neglect this detail. When I visit a congregation, I am always on the lookout for that person who will ask me for a phone number or email address to follow up with me. I stay especially cognizant for this behavior in pastors and other ministry staff and leadership. For a church member to ask me, a visitor, for my contact information proves to me that this person is serious about getting to know me. I do not know too many people who have such a magical, charismatic personality that one casual meeting with them makes you walk away thinking, " I want to change my life and accept God—or at least draw closer to him and make this church my permanent spiritual home!" I would also be hard pressed to find anyone who would possess a full understanding or comprehension of any communiqué's delivered to them verbally in one meeting or brief conversation. A prudent and experienced person will always follow-up.

However, we must pause to consider what message we are sending when we make NO effort to follow up with a guest or member of our own ministry regarding a specific sample of significant information for that matter. Our effort to create a fruitful follow-up opportunity—whether it is to make some kind of request of a new person or talk to him or her about our faith—will determine the degree to which we Christians fulfill our mandate to reach out others. In my own experience as a ministry leader, I have consistently trained young ministers to ask for a phone number or e-mail from visitors to our church or specific ministry activity. It is very difficult to follow-up with someone without any contact information! The worst they can or will do is say, "no thank you". A point to remember is that the goal of effective evangelism is not to please or impress the person in question, but to please God by fulfilling our mission to share our faith effectively. You will find that many who come out to visit a ministry event will communicate more freely and effectively in a social/personal setting outside of the said ministry activity. This is what it means to build a relationship with someone. In the same way, trying to communicate logistical details or personal information with someone will gain much more traction long term with diligent follow-up communication. To conclude this section, I would like to cite an excellent example of follow-up in the gospels. In Luke 10:1-17, Jesus sends out 72 of his followers on a short missionary journey with very specific instructions. When all the disciples return from their mission, they immediately return to Jesus with news and data from their journey. Jesus then continues to teach and give more instruction! The information I am giving here, regarding follow-up as a staple discipline in your ministry communications, is not a new concept. You will find not only examples of Jesus using this but Paul was excellent at this as well. One example was Paul's return on 3 different missionary journey's to the churches he had already established! Each trip was to teach further, appoint new leaders and just fellowship in general. Paul spent time establishing his churches, then spent the rest of his life up until the point of his imprisonment following up with those churches.

CHAPTER 25

Small Group Evangelism

A Closer, more exhaustive Look

In this chapter I would like to elaborate more exhaustively upon my personal convictions about small-group ministry and evangelism. I have developed these views based on twenty years of study and experience both as a Christian and a former campus minister.

I will open this section with a few points to emphasize before I dive deeper into a more detailed discussion of the major precepts below. In addition, I will use Matthew 11:19 as the point of reference and backdrop for my writing in this particular section of text.

19 The Son of Man came eating and drinking, and they say, 'Here is a glutton and a drunkard, a friend of tax collectors and sinners.' But wisdom is proved right by her deeds."

- I believe that effective evangelism stems from one's ability to sincerely make a "friend". If you look at the text here in Matthew 11:19, you will see that Jesus allowed himself to get so close to people that he had to unjustly endure their reputation himself. The scripture says specifically that he became a "friend" to these people who were usually looked down upon socially, morally and spiritually. This quality stands in stark contrast to the "prima dona" , elitist and exclusive outlook many "Christians" have of these same type of people. As we live in a day and age of social and political coalitions to ban, censor and ostracize those we feel are "morally below us as 'Christians', Jesus did the exact opposite by embracing people of questionable character by giving himself first in friendship before all else.

- I believe Jesus teaches us that if you cannot make a friend, you cannot make a disciple (Matt. 11:19). Recidivism relies in large part also on the ability to make and nurture friendships. If you look closely at the examples of people Jesus personally converted and kept close to him, you will find that Jesus already had some kind of bond or tie to them through a direct or indirect relationship. Such examples of this very point are: Mary Magdalene, the Apostles who were either sent to Jesus via John the Baptist or a relative such as Peter by Andrew, etc…You will find that, although Jesus preached to the masses at large, he converted people one heart and relationship at a time.

My experience is that the "friendship-making" process is most effectively facilitated on the "small group" or local "Bible talk" level. What happens on this tier will have a direct and sizeable impact on the general atmosphere and social ambiance of the church as a corporate whole. As the church is considered the Body of Christ, so the body is made up of "cells". These "cells" are the small groups led by trained and trustworthy men and women. Most churches fail to see the importance of growing on a local level and tend to focus on the "corporate" body at large. However, neglecting the local stratum eventually leads to stagnation, cold and impersonal fellowship, and cliques formed around worldly concerns like position, nepotism, race, past acquaintanceship, and so forth with only a very small part of the church enjoying any kind of meaningful fellowship. In this state of affairs, visitors are more apt to come in and out without ever being noticed or acknowledged.

I firmly believe that growth in areas of maturity and membership happens most effectively in the small groups. This is also a lesson Jethro taught his son-in-law Moses in governing Israel by using the "division principle" as previously mentioned in this writing ; Exodus 18:20.

Small, "home-based" groups can provide intimate fellowship, open communication, and mentorship more effectively than the large-group setting can as I continually state this. My ultimate goal is to help ministers and pastors see the small group infrastructure as a skeletal support holding a congregational body together giving it strength and form in much the same way a skeleton functions in a literal body.

It has also been my experience that small groups are the most effective place to convert the lost, keep the saved saved, and find, train, and commission new leaders.

As small groups grow numerically and mature, they can be parsed infinitely simply by reassigning leadership as it grows. From this starting point, a ministry can thrive to such a degree that eventually it will be able to be divided into zones, sectors, and regions as just an example of logical distribution and geographic organization.

How you label your growth strategy is secondary to having a cohesive, consistent and proactive plan to handle the faithfully forecasted growth itself.

I have been a part of churches that have used this concept and experienced exponential growth within a relatively short amount of time. The concepts I am sharing are particularly effective in large churches. Larger churches and ministries, which tend to have great periods of numerical expansion, usually experience a decline.

Because of "bottlenecks" in leadership as well as lack of vision and growth strategies that choke off the potential for continued and sustained growth, there is a subsequent decline at all levels corporately. In order to ensure that this obstacle does not permanently derail your ministry endeavors, it is best to present from the very beginning—while the church is still small—the small group as the basic unit of the corporate ministry, infrastructurally speaking.

A Deeper Focus on Evangelism as a primary function of the Small Group

Effective evangelism cannot be treated as a "Christmas and Easter" event. Effective evangelism is a Christian principle and must be imbedded into the heart before it can become a lifestyle and conviction. Principle-centered evangelism can be taught only to the "heart", and only by those whose evangelism is a deep, heart-felt conviction. Effective evangelism cannot be "faked" for long.

The small groups are equally important as a mechanism to support a vibrantly evangelistic church. As people begin to come out in larger numbers, the small groups will function a s a support to convert the lost, keep the saved tied in, build maturity through teaching and discipling and promote evangelism not as a sporadic practice but as a principled way of life.

Small Group Oversight

Not enough can be said about the importance of the director of oversight for small-group ministries. Whether the oversight comes from the lead pastor or someone else, that person must be totally trustworthy and unified with the pastoral staff. In addition, he must have a strong relationship with God and possess courage and passion for the work of his specific ministry.

A ministry leader who possesses courage will not view setbacks as failures and will persevere in nurturing the ministry through good times and bad. He will approach "problems" as challenges and adopt the view that challenges present abundant opportunities for learning and growth. In other words, a ministry leader of courage will never consider ending the small-group ministry as an option. I have seen many directors posessing great talent and ability fold under pressure because the job takes so much more than talent , ability or charisma. Most of the hard work of giving oversight to a small group (collective) ministry happens behind the scenes in what some would consider the "spiritual trenches" or "back alley ways" of the church. It is in these hidden and somewhat anonymous areas of the church where the most negative as well as the most positive impact can, will and should be made. It is a place where an oversight leader(s) can get lost in the chaos of the individual lives, dramas and struggles everyone involved in the small groups have.

Building closeness and intimacy into small group ministries as a whole and individually.

Much like any relationship such as a dating, basic friendship or marriage, facilitating an environment that encourages great communication and close relationships takes a great deal of work, deliberacy and perseverance. This is no less true for a small group ministry collectively and individually.

By creating opportunities for members to draw closer to one another, the oversight director will establish a heart-centered ministry that will be a social safe haven for all. A ministry characterized by the closeness and intimacy of its members stands in stark contrast to churches that lack the social mechanisms to prevent people from hiding in anonymity and premeditated seclusion which is the sad and unfortunate norm for many congregations. However, one should not assume that intimacy leads automatically to harmony. As people share their experiences with one another and become vulnerable before the group, unsavory elements like sin and negative attitudes will be exposed. The oversight director must be able to handle tricky situations that involve sensitive emotions and create an atmosphere of tolerance wherein all members will open their hearts to one another. I cannot emphasize enough how difficult this is. I will emphasize also that this is very possible and well worth the great work and perseverance it will take to foster such an environment and atmosphere within your own collective ministry(s).

The oversight director must also have the strength of character to accept both positive and negative feedback gracefully. He must also be prepared for the loneliness that often comes with being in such a precarious leadership position. The oversight director must not allow fear and paranoia to paralyze him. Instead, he must have the emotional stability to keep things in perspective—namely, that people can become very difficult to deal with and that, with the sole exception of oneself, the world is made up entirely of "other people".

To conclude, an oversight director must have more qualities than charisma and native talent. He must also possess the energy and discipline to carry out administrative tasks, the skill to communicate effectively with others, and a great reserve of spiritual strength and "grit" to keep him in good stead when waters get rough. The Book of Acts offers an anecdote that underscores this point. In the beginning of the book, the apostles need someone to lead the very volatile Jerusalem church. Instead of appointing one of their own—namely Peter, to whom Jesus had given the keys to the Kingdom—they appoint John, a non-apostle as evidenced in Acts 15 for his numerous leadership roles and responsibilities. This evidence leads me to believe speculatively that John was a great administrator, organizer and facilitator.

Something must have appealed to Peter and the apostles to appoint John as the leader of the Jerusalem church while they themselves demurred!

The oversight director must also be faithful and patient enough to train new leaders regularly, no matter what the climate within the ministry may be at any given time. In other words, the oversight director must have the emotional stability to carry out tasks essential to the ministry's long-term sustainability in times of disappointment as well as times of jubilation.

A small group oversight director/ minister must insist and enforce that the Bible be the core text of a ministry's foundation, teaching and spiritual standard. In the section below, I want to expound upon my conviction in this matter by presenting a few conceptually simple and pragmatic points enforcing the idea of using the bible (alone) as a proprietary form of spiritual foundation, teaching and communication for any Christian small group ministry:

1. The Bible creates a proprietary form of communication between all groups and ministries.
2. The Bible streamlines the building and communication process essential for aggressive growth locally at the small group levels as well as corporately on the congregational levels.
3. The Bible sets the standard by which all new ideas, philosophies and teachings can be measured.
4. The Bible establishes a rational system for evaluating oversight mechanisms.
5. The Bible binds all groups and ministries together cohesively regardless of their specific focus, logistical makeup or size.

I established these simple points because, without a disciplined focus and adherence to establishing the Bible as your sole spiritual foundation, others will bring their own ideas on "spiritual" teachings. With so many creative and intelligent leaders, without your biblical core established, you will see a litany of other ideas such as: myths, opinions, multi denominational and philosophical curriculums', etc being introduced to fill any gap left by lack of planning, focus and enforcement of the bible as your core source and foundation.

CHAPTER 26

Caution: Things to Beware Of

Legalism

It is very easy to get caught up in technicalities to the point that the letter of a ministry's governing principles overshadows the spirit and life of the ministry. Anything can become legalistic. Even protocols formed for the purpose of benevolence and protection can become obsessive and constricting with regard to its rules and methodologies. Maintaining the excitement, energy, and creativity within a ministry can be difficult to balance against keeping order. The key is to re-evaluate rules and procedures regularly. As the ministry grows, its needs and demands will evolve as well. This organic dynamism creates the opportunity for a ministry's latent talent and creativity to become active. Many times legalism is rooted not so much in a ministry's structure as in the way guidelines are implemented and enforced. This dynamic combined with a lack of accountability for the said protocol, or by-law, additions can easily lead to legalism.

When leader(s) become self-absorbed and self-indulgent making the ministry revolve around their own personalities and limitations, the focus on God and His people begins to suffer.

Each person is unique and brings something original to a ministry. A prudent ,wise and humble ministry leader never underestimates the importance of adapting his personal management style to accommodate the personalities, abilities and mannerisms comprising that specific ministry. Too many ministry leaders work to propagate the opposite dynamic of forcing conformity to his/ her own style, ideals and mandates of their ministry , thereby setting up an almost "cult-like" dependence on a ministry leader to be the driving life force and spiritual aggregator behind the ministry. Too many leaders see themselves as the main focus regarding the life and direction of a ministry rather than a facilitator bringing people into a synergistic communion with God and His word thus letting that fruitful dynamic drive the ministry in question forward and upward.

Being a "good shepherd" has many different responsibilities. Among them is being a good steward of all that has been entrusted by God. However, human hearts and their interaction with God as well as one another devoted to service for God are the most important thing committed to a ministry leaders' care. I say this because many ministry leaders seem to place a higher premium on logistical administration and Sunday morning theatrics (performances in service) than they do the condition of hearts in their own ministry.

Bearing this truth in mind, a ministry leader should strive for balance between being a good manager, administrator and a good shepherd. Using different strategies for maintaining order and maximizing the chances for long-term sustainability is not wrong or legalistic in and of itself; in fact, 1 Timothy 3 shows that Paul was a great proponent of orderly and proprietary worship. Systemic protocols become legalistic when they become so rigid and crystallized that adhering to them becomes and end in and of itself, to that it supersedes the spirit, the biblical focus, and the people in one's ministry. When the protocols in question stifle the organic synergy a ministry works very hard to achieve, the result is legalism.

CHAPTER 27

Discipleship/ Bringing Someone to Maturity

Help one another by facilitating an environment and atmosphere encouraging an assertive effort at developing new relationships as well as nurturing established ones.

One of the most creative and fruitful endeavors an effective leader can and should embark upon in growing his/ her ministry is facilitating opportunities for relationship -building within the ministry. The bible has a number of "one another" scriptures highlighting the different relationship interactions one should expect from a healthy and vibrant fellowship. The following are some examples I have found of "one another" scriptures in the bible:

"One Another" Exhortations of the Bible
(New International Version)

Ge 42:21 -

They said to one another, "Surely we are being punished because of our brother. We saw how distressed he was when he pleaded with us for his life, but we would not listen; that's why this distress has come upon us."

Le 19:11 -

'"Do not steal. '"Do not lie. '"Do not deceive one another.

Zec 7:9 -

"This is what the Lord Almighty says: 'Administer true justice; show mercy and compassion to one another.

Joh 13:14 -

Now that I, your Lord and Teacher, have washed your feet, you also should wash one another's feet.

Joh 13:34 -

"A new command I give you: Love one another. As I have loved you, so you must love one another.

Joh 13:35 -

By this all men will know that you are my disciples, if you love one another."

Ro 12:10 -

Be devoted to one another in brotherly love. Honor one another above yourselves.

Ro 12:16 -

Live in harmony with one another. Do not be proud, but be willing to associate with people of low position. Do not be conceited.

Ro 13:8 -

Let no debt remain outstanding, except the continuing debt to love one another, for he who loves his fellowman has fulfilled the law.

Ro 14:13 -

Therefore let us stop passing judgment on one another. Instead, make up your mind not to put any stumbling block or obstacle in your brother's way.

Ro 15:7 -

Accept one another, then, just as Christ accepted you, in order to bring praise to God.

Ro 16:16 -

Greet one another with a holy kiss. All the churches of Christ send greetings.

1Co 1:10 -

I appeal to you, brothers, in the name of our Lord Jesus Christ, that all of you agree with one another so that there may be no divisions among you and that you may be perfectly united in mind and thought.

1Co 16:20 -

All the brothers here send you greetings. Greet one another with a holy kiss.

2Co 13:12 -

Greet one another with a holy kiss.

Ga 5:13 -

You, my brothers, were called to be free. But do not use your freedom to indulge the sinful nature; rather, serve one another in love.

Eph 4:2 -

Be completely humble and gentle; be patient, bearing with one another in love.

Eph 4:32 -

Be kind and compassionate to one another, forgiving each other, just as in Christ God forgave you.

Eph 5:19 -

Speak to one another with psalms, hymns and spiritual songs. Sing and make music in your heart to the Lord,

Eph 5:21 -

Submit to one another out of reverence for Christ.

Col 3:13 -

Bear with each other and forgive whatever grievances you may have against one another. Forgive as the Lord forgave you.

Col 3:16 -

Let the word of Christ dwell in you richly as you teach and admonish one another with all wisdom, and as you sing psalms, hymns and spiritual songs with gratitude in your hearts to God.

1Th 5:11 -

Therefore encourage one another and build each other up, just as in fact you are doing.

Heb 3:13 -

But encourage one another daily, as long as it is called Today, so that none of you may be hardened by sin's deceitfulness.

Heb 10:24 -

And let us consider how we may spur one another on toward love and good deeds.

Heb 10:25 -

Let us not give up meeting together, as some are in the habit of doing, but let us encourage one another--and all the more as you see the Day approaching.

Jas 4:11 -

Brothers, do not slander one another. Anyone who speaks against his brother or judges him speaks against the law and judges it. When you judge the law, you are not keeping it, but sitting in judgment on it.

1Pe 1:22 -

Now that you have purified yourselves by obeying the truth so that you have sincere love for your brothers, love one another deeply, from the heart.

1Pe 3:8 -

Finally, all of you, live in harmony with one another; be sympathetic, love as brothers, be compassionate and humble.

1Pe 4:9 -

Offer hospitality to one another without grumbling.

1Pe 5:5 -

Young men, in the same way be submissive to those who are older. All of you, clothe yourselves with humility toward one another, because, "God opposes the proud but gives grace to the humble."

1Pe 5:14 -

Greet one another with a kiss of love. Peace to all of you who are in Christ.

1Jo 1:7 -

But if we walk in the light, as he is in the light, we have fellowship with one another, and the blood of Jesus, his Son, purifies us from all sin.

1Jo 3:11 -

This is the message you heard from the beginning: We should love one another.

1Jo 3:23 -

And this is his command: to believe in the name of his Son, Jesus Christ, and to love one another as he commanded us.

1Jo 4:7 -

Dear friends, let us love one another, for love comes from God. Everyone who loves has been born of God and knows God.

1Jo 4:11 -

Dear friends, since God so loved us, we also ought to love one another.

1Jo 4:12 -

No one has ever seen God; but if we love one another, God lives in us and his love is made complete in us.

2Jo 1:5 -

And now, dear lady, I am not writing you a new command but one we have had from the beginning. I ask that we love one another.

A few good questions to ask yourself:

> Whether you are any kind of leader or simply a devoted member of a specific faith or fellowship: "can my ministry and personal interaction in it be characterized as a "one another", relationship driven ministry? Are new and established relationships a priority to you personally and your ministry in general?

So many churches and local ministries are so very lacking in any substantial relationship dynamics which is in directly related to the anemic and pedestrian attempts to cultivate any robust small group local ministries in many churches. Instead of having a biblical "one another" culture or environment, many churches and local ministries have more of a "I worship God for myself and don't need anyone else to interfere in my personal business. All I need is God period!". The sad truth is that I used this example of what I have seen and experienced in many churches that I have visited because I actually heard a minister say those very words when I challenged him to think about having a more aggressive form of fellowship and accountability in his church as well as his own life!

Finding creative, multi-faceted ways to bond will galvanize a ministry while the ministry sets about accomplishing specific goals. For example: hold ministry-specific functional social gatherings regularly. Organize fun, age-appropriate parties and socials for teens. Set up study sessions and social gatherings geared toward creating dating opportunities for college-aged members and offer babysitting services for married couples so that they can have date nights alone or fellowship with other married couples (babysitting will also give younger ministry members a chance to earn a few extra dollars). These are JUST a few examples of fun and creative ways to facilitate creative relationship-building opportunities in your own church or specific ministry. Only your own imagination and the ideas of other ministry members will limit the list of fruitful ways to motivate and inspire each ministry. All of this activity will facilitate desirable spiritual dynamics within the ministry. Also, each of these activities can be enhanced by the addition of evangelism, prayer, mentorship, and so forth. The main objective is to guide ministry members in doing fun activities that they already want to do or are doing on their own anyway and to demonstrate that God's kingdom is the "coolest", "hottest" and most "happening" place members of a church and ministry know. The difference between an exciting and dynamic life and ministry for your members and an ordinary one is synergy and imagination!

Be careful as to whom or what your ministry is built upon.

It is not uncommon, unfortunately, for church members to become so enamored by a specific minister and/or institutionalized by a particular ministry that these become the basis of their relationship with God. Human advice and "church doctrine" are not the proper basis for an individual's personal relationship with God. To get caught up in "cults of personality" or any cultish tendencies within a church is very dangerous and all too common in today's churches. In addition, many people depend exclusively on Sunday sermons (and Sunday school on occasion) as their ONLY time during the week when they study the Bible or meditate on the Word. Most churches unintentionally condone half-hearted participation by failing to facilitate dynamic and intimate relationships mindfully. Many churches and specific ministries also fall short in holding ministry leaders accountable for creating the conditions under which church members can engage in a sustained, consistent, and disciplined engagement in the daily practice of their faith.

Three simple rules to live by as a ministry Leader:

1. Never stop believing in people!
2. Never stop believing in people!
3. Never stop believing in people!

A leader can expect to encounter challenges as he tries to develop other leaders. Sometimes people will fall short of expectations, fail to meet expectations altogether, or even quit. However, a dedicated leader will regard each situation as a learning experience. Like everything else we Christians do for God, let his kingdom and its advancement be your motivation, and keep in mind that Jesus died on the cross to set us all free from the bond of sin. In recompense, we have all failed Him and fallen short in our part of the bargain at one time or another (Rom 3:23). Judas Iscariot's betrayal of Jesus is an extreme example of how our human weaknesses can overwhelm us even in moments of great significance for our faith. Jesus believed in Judas, accepted and chose him as an apostle, and entrusted him with the Mission knowing that Judas would turn on him at the crucial moment. People will always fall short. Be careful not to take such human behavior so personally and continue to believe in, empower and spur people on towards love and good deeds as it is stated in Hebrews 10: 24.

Everyone should have his or her own relationship with God. The quality, scope and direction of all other relationships will be a direct result of your relationship with God.

Despite the close relationships that Christians form through discipleship, fellowship and other ministry related activities, everyone is ultimately responsible for his or her own relationship with God. Many members of churches and specific ministries become so enthralled and enamored by personality and/or their ministry's established rules, procedures, and culture that they form the basis of their relationship with God on the human advice and philosophies they are taught or the strength of personalities they see doing the majority of "public" leading. This very dangerous and corrosive dynamic is all too common in today's churches. Lack of emphasis, discipling and accountability on a local small group level usually perpetuates this problem.

Nurture people. Help established and potential leaders to grow by building them up gently, consistently and spiritually.

Satan and this world are always at work breaking people down and trying to negate the message of hope and reconciliation the Lord works very hard to advance. Christians, and more specifically, leaders trying to develop other leaders, should make it a practice to encourage, show kindness, and remind others of God's love, even while challenging people to take their relationship with God to another level they never thought possible. The most effective way to spread this message to others is to glorify God in every deliberation and interaction as stated so well in Proverbs 15:23, an apt and timely reply or comment are always a great way to create inroads for any conversation about your faith in God. This degree of commitment counteracts Satan's power, which is not rooted in the supernatural but in the discipline, persistence and consistency with which he works against God and His Kingdom.

CHAPTER 28

Seek first the His Word!

As humans, we are plagued with the flaw of always trying to "fix" people with our "wisdom" and philosophical prowess. I do believe that people can and should speak from the heart on matters, but I would caution that spiritual matters be handled better by nudging people toward God's word in a gentle and loving way as their primary source of wisdom and council. Encouraging a non-Christian to see what God says on a given subject and then consider the input of fellow seekers of God is yet another way to lead someone to the Truth in a gentle, loving, and supportive manner. In this situation, the Bible will act as an "axis" that links differing spiritual views.

A leader who is skillful in steering people toward God's word will also give new converts to the faith time and space to work through spiritual dilemmas and struggles with God. Crisis can be a catalyst for the development of spiritual maturity. Imagine a whole ministry of people doing this consistently with one another!

Conflict is another major challenge for many leaders on all levels. I have seen so many situations in which leaders distance themselves from internecine disagreements. I have seen leaders send subordinates to resolve a situation and report back on the results. I have seen leaders just ignore situations that demand a meeting or confrontation. I have seen leaders use their pulpit or another public forum to denounce certain goings-on and discredit people who have valid disagreements and grievances as unspiritual, sinful and ungrateful, with the end result being that people are intimidated to express criticism, air concerns, and deal with problems openly and honestly. Make no mistake: to use the power of the pulpit to suppress dissent is a very serious form of manipulation with cultish undertones. As long as things can be resolved in an orderly way, in a manner that does not unduly disrupt the ministry; a spiritual leader should welcome feedback—whether it be positive or negative. The outcome could very well be personal and spiritual growth for the person being evaluated. In my experiences, some of my most loyal friends and supporters began as my staunchest critics. This advice, however, does not pertain to situations in which a person wants to malign, publically embarrass, or subvert a ministry. In those cases, the person must be dealt with in keeping with the Bible's instruction in how to handle divisiveness, dissention, factions, and other destructive devices introduced into the body through unscrupulous men (2 Pet 2: 1-22 NIV). I feel strongly that there is a distinct difference between someone who has a valid grievance with a leader and wants to resolve things biblically and expeditiously and a person or persons who simply want to "poison" a ministry with no intention of reconciliation. It is important that an experienced leader(s) be able to discern between the two dynamics and handle with great wisdom and maturity. Too many leaders try to avoid any kind of grievance or conflict altogether through suppression and/ or deflection. As in any family, there will be disagreements. Have the courage to handle them and accept them as a natural and spiritual part of the life of your specific ministry.

CHAPTER 29

Ministry Maintenance

A ministry leader will have to work. Nothing in this writing has suggested otherwise. One of my main goals in writing this book is offer guidance to ministry leadership with an aim toward bringing greater focus, clarity, and efficiency to a ministry leader's daily work. The following are some suggestions for routine tasks and practices that will keep a ministry's "engine" humming so as to avoid as many major breakdowns as possible—at least those brought about by laziness, complacency, irresponsibility, and ignorance.

Finding and keeping the fires of the spirit hot during "grind" times in your ministry through daily discipling and relationship-building. Finding a way to combat monotony and stagnation.

Satan never lets up! Let me repeat that: Satan NEVER lets up. He never sleeps or tires. He never lacks in zeal or motivation. He lives to destroy God's Kingdom one believer at a time with leaders at the top of that "hit list". He follows up daily to make sure that God's forward progress in each of our lives is hampered in every possible way. Likewise, a good ministry leader fights "fire with fire" by following up with the members of his ministry so as to keep the Spirit of God advancing in their lives. A ministry leader can safely assume his people are having more challenging days than encouraging ones. With that in mind, encouraging people with a phone call, e-mail, or text can go a long way toward motivating them to stay on the path of righteousness. The key to successful follow up is that it is daily and consistent. Fruitful follow up is also genuine and sincere for the true leader with a heart for his/ her people.

Just as Jesus was always teaching about God, a good ministry leader, armed with the knowledge and wisdom afforded him by God's spirit, will work tirelessly toward the perpetuation of God's message by teaching others to teach others.

I once heard it said (in a very apt oversimplification) that a leader's job boils down to one basic task: to remind people constantly that they are awesome and God loves them. There is a lot of truth and substance in this simplified view of a leader's main job. Both the Bible and life are full of "reminders that we are awesome and that God loves us". A good leader will let no one with whom he has significant contact go "un-reminded"!

A good leader will find creative ways not only to offer his service, but to encourage others to serve, as well. For example: if a single mom, elderly person, or person with a disability in one's ministry needs some help with yard work, a good ministry leader will ask some of the brothers who have time on a Saturday to help her out. To provide a little extra incentive, one might buy the young men a pizza and sodas after they have completed their work. Service should be celebratory, joyful, thoughtful and creative. One caveat of this service-centered approach is that in order for it to work, it requires personal interaction and communication. Without these, it will be difficult to know who and how people in one's ministry need to be served. It will also be difficult to keep track of those with the time, ability and motivation to go the extra mile in serving.

It is important, especially for men, to be deliberate in building relationships with others in the ministry. To use Jesus as an example, the first thing He did after coming out of the desert was to build relationships with the fist apostles he called to follow him. The Lord proved by his actions that relationships were of paramount importance to him and his ministry.

> Much like the old saying,
> "the best defense is a good offense",
> Growth is the best maintenance
> program for any ministry.

A good ministry leader will build relationships in accordance with his overall vision for his ministry. Being genuine with each individual one contacts, reminding ministry members of how valuable they are to the specific ministry of which they are a part, recognizing each person's unique contribution to the advancement of the ministry's program and facilitating opportunities to serve are just a few synergistic ways to generate a sense of collective ownership and excitement. People will work and work hard for God if they feel—by constantly being reminded—that leadership values their efforts and recognizes the difference they make.

CHAPTER 30

Keeping "Self" in Check and Accountable

In my many years of studying corporate and small group church and specific ministry dynamics, another disturbing trend have I encountered repeatedly.

I have added this section because of the ramifications of a particular type of leader. This particular leader will usually distance himself from any thought of small groups, greater distribution of leadership authority and responsibility and many of the other ministry dynamics discussed in this writing that would lead to a more dynamic, robust and synergistic ministry both collectively and locally. This type of leader will strive to keep leadership authority in a controlled vacuum, exclusive and corporately centralized.

Many churches and local ministries fall victim to over-opportunistic ministry staff and leaders who see their respective ministries as a means by which to climb the "corporate church ladder" in hopes of attaining a more prestigious title, higher paying salary, greater sphere of administrative influence and ascension in the hierarchical chain of leadership.

These days, when talented leaders are dissatisfied with their church, they often respond by starting their own. This dynamic can be evidenced by the vast number, denominationally differentiated and ethno-culturally segregated churches that are not only in existence, but that seem to breed new start-ups daily.

Alarmingly, a state of affairs in which so many people start their own ministries in order to gratify their ego stretches scriptural parameters to the point of heresy just to appease the strong urges brought about by ego and vindication. In this particular segment, I am speaking specifically of the many potential leaders who seek a full-time ministry position assuming that such a position or title is a validation of spiritual ordainment combined with vocational professionalism. Moreover, many smaller churches want to emulate larger churches in their view of God's people more as financial contributors rather than as precious souls to be trained in God's service. Many place personal financial ambitions for ministry ahead of Godly ambitions and therefore make the potential financial gain of ministering the primary criterion for how, where, when they will serve. Anyone whose motivation for ministering is primarily to acquire a full-time, salaried position should consider the consequences of using a spiritual mission to achieve worldly ends. What happened regarding the birth of the Holy Roman Church/Empire under Constantine in the mid-300s A.D is such an example where church authority became salaried, centralized, dogmatic, political, legally ordained and entitled through a new and secular crystallization of church polity. As a counter-example, one might revisit the story of the apostle Paul, who held a full-time job while he was doing the Lord's work; and Barnabas, who gave his own wealth to the church so that he could work full time as a minister for God's church. In addition, Paul and Barnabas both strived to appoint leaders (elders) in plurality to each local congregation they encountered, built or strengthened to take on the local work of leading. Paul and the other founding fathers of the modern church displayed more than enough ability to establish mega-church situations in which they could have "ruled" and become wealthy themselves, yet did not! A pure heart for God and His ministry will fight this temptation. The irony to all of this is that the opposite heart displayed by Paul and his contemporaries for selfless and sacrificial leadership seems to the accepted norm regarding modern day ministry vocational ambitions and motives.

A good ministry leader will actively guard against letting his ego control his motivation to lead and leadership style. This is not to say he will not struggle with it. An experienced and informed ministry leader will be fully aware of the battle to contain ego and plan for it. Specific strategies can include but not be limited to building consensus for major decisions, getting people involved in the ministry's overarching vision and daily work, and giving others the opportunity to shine by taking responsibility for significant areas of church/ ministry development. Giving God all glory is a foregone conclusion, but allowing others to be lifted up for successes, even if a leader has to take a back seat, does wonders for keeping his ego in check and keeping God in plain view. Pride, arrogance, and self-reliance can impede one's view and overall relationship with God. When a leader proactively seeks opportunities to shift the glory elsewhere, he preserves the overall condition of his own heart. As a leader, one of the most challenging things you can do to keep your heart in check is to continue to play a significant role in developing your ministry while deliberately looking for ways to remain anonymous in the process quickly and proactively shifting glory to God and others. This is a conviction I have come to over many years of leading knowing fully how easily my heart gives into the seductive trap of ego.

Look for opportunities and cherish them when they happen regarding having your heart and motives tested as a leader in service for God. The fruit of a receptive heart will lead to salvation for both yourself and those who listen to you-I Timothy 4:16.

A leader should pray for God to give him opportunities to see his heart and expose his motives. To see one's own flaws and face one's weaknesses is not an exciting or comfortable prospect, but in my own experience, I have been grateful when God sent other people and set up challenges that fortified the ministry's health and protected it when I accepted criticism with humility and faced challenges head on. Many times the greatest threats to a ministry are not outside circumstances, but arrogance, ego, and selfish, worldly ambitions on the part of leadership. These can destroy a ministry from within. In my many years of observation, when I have seen the downfall of a church or ministry, it was usually brought about by problems within leadership and not any outside forces, persecution or upheavals in the general congregational membership.

A balanced leader finds a way to effectively process input from others while finding opportunities to learn and nurture discipling relationships as well.

It can be challenging for a leader to strike an ideal balance between being easily approachable and open to other's input and standing one's ground when it becomes necessary to defend one's deep convictions when one is challenged or comes "under fire". I believe each circumstance will yield its own solutions. Through prayer and seeking the counsel of both the Bible and trusted advisors, one can balance approachability and principled intransigence. In the end, one will find clarity in the "middle". One may find great strength and wisdom in the passage of text in the Old Testament, Ecclesiastes 7:8-20, which states:

The end of a matter is better than its beginning,
  and patience is better than pride.
9 Do not be quickly provoked in your spirit,
  for anger resides in the lap of fools.

10 Do not say, "Why were the old days better than these?"
For it is not wise to ask such questions.
11 Wisdom, like an inheritance, is a good thing
and benefits those who see the sun.
12 Wisdom is a shelter
as money is a shelter,
but the advantage of knowledge is this:
Wisdom preserves those who have it.
13 Consider what God has done:
Who can straighten
what he has made crooked?
14 When times are good, be happy;
but when times are bad, consider this:
God has made the one
as well as the other.
Therefore, no one can discover
anything about their future.
15 In this meaningless life of mine I have seen both of these:
the righteous perishing in their righteousness,
and the wicked living long in their wickedness.
16 Do not be overrighteous,
neither be overwise—
why destroy yourself?
17 Do not be overwicked,
and do not be a fool—
why die before your time?
18 It is good to grasp the one

and not let go of the other.
Whoever fears God will avoid all extremes.
19 Wisdom makes one wise person more powerful
than ten rulers in a city.
20 Indeed, there is no one on earth who is righteous,
no one who does what is right and never sins.

Always keep a balanced perspective when receiving input, process patiently and embrace the opportunity to learn. A mature and spiritual leader understands that he is never beyond or above reproach by anyone.

A ministry leader who puts himself and his own needs above the overall good of his ministry and tries to hide or deny it (ego) is like a naked man running through the streets completely oblivious, bragging to everyone about his fine new clothes he is now wearing.-Chris Perkins

A good minister knows that he cannot do everything alone. Most everything done can be done more effectively in teams or groups. The Gospels in the first four books of the New Testament bible are littered with examples showing that Jesus rarely did anything alone save His own devotional time with God. We ministry leaders should be humbled by the fact that the Son of God—who could do all things—modeled the importance of building relationships with people who could help with God's work . Jesus always parceled out responsibilities to his men fully trusting them to carry out their directives. I would like to add an extra point to punctuate Jesus' belief in His men and the extent to which He went to delegate responsibility: He even trusted Judas knowing fully that he was the betrayer that would eventually set in motion the events leading up to the crucifixion of our Lord Jesus!

What is best for the ministry is always simplicity, enforcement and consistency. Most importantly, a ministry must be led by a person with a heart that is willing to change in whatever way necessary for the advancement of God's kingdom. In extreme situations, this may include stepping down or out of the way to make room for someone whose heart can be more effective for God during a particular season. Philippians 2:1-18 gives us a great example of the enormous amount of humility Jesus displayed as the Son of God to relate to us as people. Jesus came with a purpose to lead by serving as seen in Matthew 20:28 which states:

"just as the Son of Man did not come to be served, but to serve, and to give his life as a ransom for many."

A good ministry leader will celebrate the successes of others and let others be glorified. This magnanimity helps to keep the heart pure. Experience has convinced me that an effective minister/ leader will eventually "work himself out of a job"—that is, he will create the conditions for the ministry to continue in his absence facilitating and empowering others to take responsibility and ownership of their own collective ministries'. I personally never see ministry as a job or vocation because that is not the heart I see in the bible of those who decide to follow in the footsteps of Jesus as a leader in God's service. I see ministry leadership as a journey and myself as just one small part of it. I have always had a difficult time believing that someone would be able to maintain a truly spiritual condition of heart (knowing all too well humans sinful nature) when he makes himself out to be the "main character" in a "story" that actually holds eternal ramifications for countless numbers of people. I have joyfully given up my position several times to more effective leaders whom I had personally trained for leadership. For me, it is all about God's kingdom going as far as it can, regardless of my role in it. God can use anyone. It would behoove every leader to keep in mind that his or her personal position or status alone will not determine the final outcome of God's kingdom. I am also a firm believer that a spiritual leader is always taking into account (1 John 4:1) the condition of his/ her own heart. A good leader has the integrity to save his ministry by saving himself if he should ever come to the realization that God is no longer the sole motivation for his endeavors (Rev. 3:16).

CHAPTER 31

Conclusion

My purpose in writing this book has been to provoke thought and self-reflection with an ultimate aim toward facilitating creative momentum. As a ministry leader or potential ministry leader, one will find oneself not only on a journey through his own life and the lives of his members, but also on an exploration and discovery of the human heart. Sometimes we get so caught up in the administrative responsibilities of leading our ministries that we fail to nurture and develop that which is most important: the heart of each individual member and the heart of the collective, as well.

The reader who has reached the end of this book has taken an important step on the road to developing his ministry from a proactive—rather than a reactive—position. Contemplate all that I have written here, meditate on the points that are most pertinent to your situation, and seek God's wisdom in regard to adapting the principles and strategies I have outlined here for your specific ministry situation. Devise creative ways to bring people to God and keep them excited about working for his Kingdom. My ultimate hope is that you are able to use my suggestions to refine your approach and enhance your ambition to lead effectively and joyfully in God's service.

CPSIA information can be obtained
at www.ICGtesting.com
Printed in the USA
BVHW01s2122101217
502436BV00001B/77/P

9 781506 900445